YOU CAN GO BANKRUPT WITHOUT GOING BROKE

YOU CAN GO BANKRUPT WITHOUT GOING BROKE

An Essential Guide
to Personal Bankruptcy

LAWRENCE R. REICH and JAMES P. DUFFY

BeardBooks
Washington, D.C.

Copyright © 1992 by Lawrence R. Reich and James P. Duffy
Reprinted 2003 by Beard Books, Washington, D.C.

Library of Congress Cataloging-in-Publication Data

Reich, Lawrence R.
  You can go bankrupt without going broke : an essential guide to personal bankruptcy / by Lawrence R. Reich, James P. Duffy.
    p. cm.
Originally published: New York : Pharos books, 1992.
Includes index.
ISBN : 1-58798-209-9
  1. Bankruptcy--United States--Popular works. 2. Debtor and creditor--United States--Popular works. I. Duffy, James P., 1941 - II Title.

KF1524.6.R45 2003
346.7307'8--dc22

2003052397

This publication is designed to provide accurate and authoritative information in regard to the subject matter covered at the time it was written. It is sold with the understanding that the publisher is not engaged in rendering legal, accounting, or other professional service. If legal advice or other expert assistance is required, the services of a competent professional person should be sought.

    —From a Declaration of Principles jointly adopted by a Committee of the American Bar Association and a Committee of Publishers.

Printed in the United States of America

All rights reserved. No part of this publication may be reproduced or transmitted in any form, by any means, electronic or mechanical, including photocopy, recording, or any information storage or retrieval system, without permission in writing from the publisher.

To the memory of
Sidney H. Reich

Contents

Acknowledgments xiv

ONE   WHEN IT'S TIME TO FACE THE FACTS   1

    Bankruptcy Through the Ages   2
        The Acceptance of Credit and Debt   3
        The Purpose of Bankruptcy Laws   5
        The Role of Bankruptcy Courts   5

    Financial Warning Signs   6
        Questions to Ask Yourself   6
        What Your Next Step Should Be   8

    Bankruptcy as a Way Out   9
        What Bankruptcy Can and Cannot Do for You   9
        "How Did I Get to This Point?"   10
        Three Profiles in Bankruptcy   11

TWO   DEBTORS HAVE RIGHTS, KNOW YOURS   17

    Consumer Protection Laws   18
        The Truth in Lending Act   18
        The Equal Credit Opportunity Act   19
        The Fair Credit Billing Act   20
        The Fair Credit Reporting Act   20
        The Fair Debt Collection Practices Act   21

Contents

Consumer Reporting Agencies and Your Credit File 22
What's in Your Credit File 23
How to Check Your Credit File 25
What to Do if You Are Refused Credit 27
How to Correct Your Credit File 28
How to Resolve Billing Disputes 30

Dealing with Debt Collectors 32
What Debt Collectors Can Do 33
What Debt Collectors Can't Do 33
What Debtors Can Do 34

Dealing with the Internal Revenue Service 36
The Taxpayer Bill of Rights 37
What the IRS Must Do 38
What a Taxpayer Can Do 38

Always Be Protected and Prepared 39

THREE   FINDING ALTERNATIVES TO BANKRUPTCY 41

When Bankruptcy Will Not Work 41
If Your Debts Are Secured 41
If You Had a Previous Bankruptcy 44
If You Are Judgment Proof 44
Other Reasons Not to File Bankruptcy 45

When and How to Settle Out of Court 46
How to Negotiate with Your Creditors 47
Use an Assignment for Benefit of Creditors 48

Where to Find Help 48
The Truth About Consumer Counseling Services 50
Using a Bankruptcy Attorney 52
A Do-It-Yourself Bankruptcy 53

Contents

FOUR   HOW TO GET YOUR CREDITORS TO SETTLE FOR LESS   54

Determining How Much You Can Pay   54
Simple Financial Formulas   54
Selecting the Right Creditors   56

Contacting Your Creditors   58
Meeting Your Creditor Face to Face   59

FIVE   WHEN BANKRUPTCY IS THE ONLY WAY OUT   66

Classifying Your Debts   66
Dischargeable Debts   69
Nondischargeable Debts   71
Debts That May Be Nondischargeable   72

The Advantages of Personal Bankruptcy   74
Stop Creditors from Harassing You   74
Protect Your Property   74
Control Your Dealings with Creditors   75
Halt Legal Action by Creditors   75

The Disadvantages of Personal Bankruptcy   79
You May Lose Your Property   79
How It Will Affect Your Mortgage   80
What Happens to Your Credit Standing   81
The Impact on Your Future Credit   82
About Your Personal Reputation   83

Your Next Step   84
Get Competent Help   85

Bankruptcy, Chapter by Chapter   85
Selecting the Right Chapter   87

Contents

SIX   WHAT YOU SHOULD KNOW ABOUT CHAPTER 7 BANKRUPTCY   89

Deciding If Chapter 7 Is Right for You   89
 When to Use Chapter 7   90
 Who Is Eligible for Chapter 7   90

The Chapter 7 Filing   90
 When to File Chapter 7   90
 What Is Filed   91
 What the Court Fees Are   91

The Chapter 7 Process   92
 What the Bankruptcy Trustee Does   92
 How Creditors Are Notified   92
 The Meeting of Your Creditors   93
 Questions You Must Answer   93
 Asset and No-Asset Cases   95

The Resolution of Your Filing   96
 How Your Debts Are Discharged   96
 What Happens After the Discharge   96
 Why Your Case Could Be Dismissed   96
 How to Deal with Secured Creditors   97
 Why You Should Refuse to Sign a Reaffirmation Agreement   98

SEVEN   WHAT YOU SHOULD KNOW ABOUT CHAPTER 11 BANKRUPTCY   101

Deciding If Chapter 11 Is Right for You   101
 Who Is Eligible for Chapter 11   101
 The Advantages of Chapter 11   102
 Who Chapter 11 Helps   102

The Chapter 11 Process   103
 How Court Fees Are Set   103
 Developing a Payment Plan   103
 How Your Plan Is Approved   104

Contents

EIGHT WHAT YOU SHOULD KNOW ABOUT CHAPTER 12 BANKRUPTCY 106

Deciding If Chapter 12 Is Right for You 106
  Who Is Eligible for Chapter 12 107
  The Advantages of Chapter 12 107

The Chapter 12 Process 107
  How Co-signers Are Protected 107
  Your Repayment Period 108
  How Creditors Are Treated 108

NINE WHAT YOU SHOULD KNOW ABOUT CHAPTER 13 BANKRUPTCY 109

Deciding If Chapter 13 Is Right for You 109
  When to Use Chapter 13 109
  The Advantages of Chapter 13 111
  The Disadvantages of Chapter 13 112
  Who Is Eligible for Chapter 13 113

The Chapter 13 Filing 114
  About Your Payment Plan 114
  Your Filing Costs 114

The Chapter 13 Process 115
  What the Bankruptcy Trustee Does 115
  Your Employer May Be Notified 115
  How Creditors Are Notified 116
  How a Payment Plan Is Established 116
  What Happens When Your Creditors Meet 117
  Your Confirmation Hearing 118
  If Your Plan Is Not Confirmed 118

The Chapter 13 Discharge 118
  How Secured Creditors Are Treated 119
  What to Do If Your Plan Fails 120
  When to Request a Hardship Discharge 120

Contents

TEN   YOUR EXEMPTIONS: FROM ALABAMA TO WYOMING   121

ELEVEN   HOME AND REAL ESTATE EXEMPTIONS: A STATE-BY-STATE GUIDE   173

TWELVE   WHY YOU SHOULD CONSIDER USING AN ATTORNEY   180
- The Attorney's Roles   181
  - *As Your Advisor*   181
  - *As Your Negotiator*   182
  - *As Your Representative*   183
- How to Find a Personal Bankruptcy Attorney   184
  - *How to Select the Right Attorney*   185

THIRTEEN   HOW YOU CAN PROTECT YOUR ASSETS   188
- Plan Ahead for Best Results   188
  - *Plan Well in Advance of Your Filing*   189
  - *Keep the "Pig Theory" in Mind*   189
  - *Stay Within the Applicable Laws*   190
- Important Steps You Can Take   191
  - *How to Convert Nonexempt Property Legally to Exempt Property*   191
  - *How to Use Nonexempt Property to Pay Off Nondischargeable Debts*   194
  - What You Should Not Do   195

FOURTEEN   YOUR LIFE AFTER BANKRUPTCY   198
- Reestablishing Your Charge Accounts   200
  - *Use the Charge Accounts You Saved*   200
  - *How to Use Secured Credit Cards*   202

Contents

Use Bank Accounts for Credit 205
    Take Out a Passbook Loan 205
    Debit Cards Will Help You 205
    Apply for a Secured Loan 206

Protect Your New Credit 206
    Keep Your Credit Files Clean 206
    A Final Warning 207

A GLOSSARY OF TERMS YOU SHOULD KNOW 208

Appendix A   FEDERAL BANKRUPTCY EXEMPTIONS 212

Appendix B   SAMPLE BANKRUPTCY FORMS 215

INDEX 235

Acknowledgments

Special thanks are due to Martha V. Moran and Avda K. Bartsch for their very able assistance and also for the support of my wife, Madeline, and our children, Robin and Jeffrey, without whose support this endeavor would not have been possible.

L.R.R.

Once again I owe thanks to my good friend Vince Ricci for his contribution to this book, to my wife, Kathleen, for her support, and to Alexandra and Olivia, who make everything worthwhile.

J.P.D.

One

WHEN IT'S TIME TO FACE THE FACTS

If you are faced with mounting credit card bills, unexpected medical bills beyond your ability to pay, the failure of a business into which you sank all your savings and every dollar you could borrow, long-term unemployment or underemployment which forced you to dip into your savings for normal living expenses, or any of a thousand other circumstances that may have left you with more expenses and debts than you think you can realistically repay, you might be a candidate for personal bankruptcy.

Not everyone with financial difficulties is a bankruptcy candidate. Although personal bankruptcy no longer carries the social stigma it once did, when you file for bankruptcy, you will acquire burdens with which you will have to live for years to come. While under the strain of pressing debts you might feel you are willing to bear those burdens, it is critical that you examine all options before deciding on a course of action.

In the following chapters we provide all the information required to consider bankruptcy as an alternative to your present situation. This includes explanations of the various types of personal bankruptcy, the alternatives to bankruptcy,

You *Can* Go Bankrupt *Without* Going Broke

where to get help and where you may not want to get help, the impact bankruptcy will have on your future, how the bankruptcy courts function, and what you can expect your life to be like after your debts have been discharged in bankruptcy.

BANKRUPTCY THROUGH THE AGES

First, a little history will help you understand our modern bankruptcy laws, especially how and why they came into existence as a way of protecting debtors from being driven into destitution.

Until the Industrial Revolution radically changed our society, it was unusual for an individual to owe money to more than one creditor. Multiple creditors were a rarity. A debtor who was unable to repay his debts confronted two equally distasteful consequences. He could have all his personal belongings seized by his creditor, or he could be thrown into prison. If the value of his personal possessions was less than the amount he owed, he could face both penalties. In those somewhat primitive times, owing money was a mark of disgrace that revealed a defect in one's character.

In 1340 King Edward III of England caused two famous early bankruptcies when he defaulted on personal loans he had obtained from two wealthy Florentine families, the Bardis and the Peruzzis, and forced both families into bankruptcy.

The first English bankruptcy law on which our own is based was enacted in 1543. Although the law gave a debtor the ability to protect himself from process servers by taking refuge in a religious sanctuary or a cathedral city, or by remaining within his own house, his assets could still be seized to settle his unpaid debts.

By the mid-1700s the colony of Virginia had passed a

law that stated that a defaulting debtor could be held in prison no longer than 20 days. At that time he was required to be taken before a court where he was asked to swear an oath that he was unable to pay his debt. Having done this, the debtor's property, excluding his wearing apparel and the tools required for his trade, was seized. The debtor was then released from custody and the obligation of his debt.

A common practice in the American colonies at this time was that debtors who could not pay their debts could be imprisoned as long as their creditors paid the cost of their upkeep. In New York the creditor was required to pay three shillings per week to keep a defaulting debtor in prison.

The colony of Georgia had a statute that discharged the debts of most persons from other countries and colonies who moved to Georgia. The purpose of this law was to give newly arriving immigrants a "fresh start."

The Acceptance of Credit and Debt

When we recall how a person in default was once viewed by society, we should remember that these were times when people expected to live out their lives in the same circumstances into which they were born. Today many people have used and continue to use credit and borrowed money to improve their lives and move up the social and economic ladder. Sometimes this endeavor is wildly successful, and sometimes it invites disaster.

Countless successful businesses and great fortunes have been and continue to be spawned with borrowed money. Using credit, or borrowing money, is no longer considered the sign of a defective character. It has become the means by which an entrepreneur can build a large thriving business providing employment for thousands of others. In that sense, use of credit can allow people to reach beyond their own financial abilities to seize the dreams that might otherwise elude them.

You *Can* Go Bankrupt *Without* Going Broke

As a result of the changes brought about by industrialization, credit acquired a new respectability. People borrowed money to build new factories or expand existing ones. It was no longer a stigma to borrow money provided it was repaid, along with the interest agreed on when the loan was granted.

But what if you can't pay back the loan and the interest? What if you cannot pay anything? Thank goodness we no longer need to worry about creditors confiscating our property or having us imprisoned. Both of those actions appear designed only to punish a debtor who has gotten in over his head, not help him to climb out of the hole he is in and try to start over building a productive life.

The framers of the U.S. Constitution understood the need to handle the problems of debtors humanely, so they included a clause in Article I of the Constitution giving Congress the power to establish "uniform laws on the subject of bankruptcies throughout the United States."

Although the discharge of debts in bankruptcy became a part of American law in 1841, the first modern bankruptcy law in this country was the Bankruptcy Act of 1898. It was substantially amended and modernized in 1938 by the Chandler Act and again in 1978 by the Bankruptcy Reform Act. Additional amendments were added in 1984 and on several subsequent occasions.

The 1978 act was a complete modernization of the laws made necessary because the administrative machinery as organized under the old law could no longer keep pace with the increase in bankruptcies. Between 1948 and 1978 the number of bankruptcies in the United States increased by a whopping 1,000 percent. More people came into contact with the federal judicial system through the bankruptcy courts than through any other. In fact, the number of civil and criminal cases filed in federal courts combined doesn't even approach the number of cases filed in federal bankruptcy courts.

When It's Time to Face the Facts

An important point to keep in mind is that although state laws may impact on some portion of a bankruptcy filing, such as asset protection, which we will discuss later, bankruptcy comes under the federal laws and is handled in special courts established by the federal government.

The Purpose of Bankruptcy Laws

The bankruptcy laws under which we live are a body of rules which have the primary goal of distributing a debtor's assets equitably among the creditors. A secondary function is the collection of debts. In all but the most unusual cases, none of this is done in a way that leaves a defaulting debtor without a place to live or strips a debtor of all assets entirely.

The most fundamental purposes of the U.S. bankruptcy laws are:

1. To convert a debtor's assets into cash and distribute that cash in an equitable manner among the debtor's creditors.
2. To give the debtor an opportunity that would not otherwise be available to have a "fresh start" in life with those assets that the bankruptcy law exempts from distribution to creditors.

The Role of Bankruptcy Courts

It might help to understand the role and process of bankruptcy if we think of the bankruptcy court as a central location to which a debtor and all creditors come to settle the issues between them. It is a single proceeding in which the rights of debtors and creditors are protected and all participants are treated fairly. As a result, creditors are prevented by law from taking separate action against a person who has filed for bankruptcy, such as salary garnishment or asset seizure. Actually, filing a bankruptcy means all actions by creditors must stop and their claims consolidated in one place, the bankruptcy court.

You *Can* Go Bankrupt *Without* Going Broke

Not surprisingly, contemporary bankruptcy courts are increasingly called on to settle all sorts of issues having little to do with the traditional issues of bankruptcy, such as determining the proper role of labor unions and pension funds. Bankruptcy courts are also required to apply a variety of state and federal laws in such areas as taxes, contracts, mortgages, landlord and tenant relationships, partnerships, domestic relations, and constitutional law.

Bankruptcy gives the honest but unfortunate individual facing overwhelming debt a chance to start fresh without the burden of those debts. If you are such an individual, be assured that the bankruptcy court will prevent your creditors from stripping you of everything you own and making you destitute. The various laws are intended to leave you with sufficient assets to make a "fresh start."

Many people who file for bankruptcy do so out of a desperation brought on by an earlier reluctance to face facts. In many ways these debtors are not unlike sick people who refuse to go to a doctor because they hope that by denial, the illness will somehow become nonexistent.

FINANCIAL WARNING SIGNS

People who hope that somehow their financial problems will evaporate or be miraculously resolved blind themselves to the consequences of overwhelming debt. This is one reason that state lotteries and gambling casinos are so popular, particularly among people who don't have the resources to squander on them. The same can be said for the popularity of get-rich-quick schemes and books which claim to instruct you how to become a millionaire without having any money to start with.

Questions to Ask Yourself

Following is a short quiz that will help you determine if you

When It's Time to Face the Facts

are headed for a financial crisis. Answer each question yes or no. Before answering, search deep inside yourself to be sure you are answering each question honestly.

1. Without pulling out the latest statements, are you unaware of how much money you presently owe on all your credit cards, revolving charge accounts, and outstanding loans?
   ❏ Yes   ❏ No

2. Do you have trouble making the minimum payments on your credit accounts and loans?
   ❏ Yes   ❏ No

3. Do you have trouble making your monthly rent or mortgage payment?
   ❏ Yes   ❏ No

4. Have you used cash advances from your credit cards to pay normal routine living expenses?
   ❏ Yes   ❏ No

5. At bill-paying time, do you wonder where your money went?
   ❏ Yes   ❏ No

6. Do the monthly payments on your credit card and other consumer loans (excluding mortgage payments) exceed 25 percent of your take-home pay?
   ❏ Yes   ❏ No

7. Are you able to put even a small amount of money from each paycheck into a savings or similar account?
   ❏ Yes   ❏ No

8. Do you have to work overtime just to keep up with your monthly bills?
   ❏ Yes   ❏ No

You *Can* Go Bankrupt *Without* Going Broke

9. Do you use money reserved for other financial obligations, such as insurance or taxes, to pay monthly bills?
   ❏ Yes   ❏ No

10. Is a creditor threatening to sue you, obtain a judgment against you, or garnishee your salary?
    ❏ Yes   ❏ No

11. Are you consistently late in paying any of your bills?
    ❏ Yes   ❏ No

12. Have you recently been denied credit because of information in your credit file?
    ❏ Yes   ❏ No

13. Do you feel threatened or harassed by bills you are unable to pay?
    ❏ Yes   ❏ No

14. Are you worried that your recent bill-paying habits will result in your being evicted, your mortgage foreclosed, or your car or furniture repossessed?
    ❏ Yes   ❏ No

15. Do you live with the hope that a winning lottery ticket or the death of some unknown relative will give you the money you need to catch up with your bills?
    ❏ Yes   ❏ No

16. Will the loss of two week's pay result in your not being able to pay your bills?
    ❏ Yes   ❏ No

What Your Next Step Should Be

If you answered yes to more than half these questions, you are probably facing serious financial trouble in the near future.

Even if you answered yes to only one or two questions,

When It's Time to Face the Facts

you need to examine your current spending and life-style habits to preclude a future financial problem. While some people who are confronted with severe financial difficulties can pinpoint a primary cause, such as loss of a job, costly illness, or other family crisis, a great many feel as if the problem "crept up on me like a thief in the night," as one woman who filed bankruptcy put it.

If you answered yes to the majority of questions, don't waste time; seek professional advice regarding your finances immediately. This book is designed to help you ensure that your knowledge of the consumer protection laws, the bankruptcy laws, as well as the bankruptcy process itself are sufficient so you can make fully informed decisions when and from whom to seek advice and the value of that advice.

BANKRUPTCY AS A WAY OUT

Bankruptcy isn't a quick fix for financial difficulties. It has both short-term and long-term benefits and drawbacks that must be examined closely before you decide to file. Throughout this book we will continue to discuss these to make you fully aware of both sides of the result of filing bankruptcy. This is a brief overview of bankruptcy that will help you understand what it can accomplish for you.

What Bankruptcy Can and Cannot Do for You

1. While filing for bankruptcy will get most of your creditors off your back, you will have a hard time obtaining new credit for as long as ten years.

2. Bankruptcy will not strip you of all your possessions, but it could mean you will lose some, unless your assets are exempt or you file a Chapter 13 case (or, in certain circumstances, a Chapter 11 or 12 case) under which you may obtain time to make up arrears in past due payments through a time payment plan under which you will not lose your assets. Each case is different, and the laws of each state concerning exemptions vary.

3. Bankruptcy will not cost you your job. Usually your employer need never know you have filed bankruptcy. In any event, employers are prohibited by federal law from discriminating against a prospective employee because of a bankruptcy, but it may cost you a promotion where no one has to say why you were not promoted. In addition, discrimination against an individual who filed bankruptcy is hard to prove, even if it is illegal.

4. You should follow the instructions in this book and select a competent bankruptcy attorney. You must be honest with your attorney and with the bankruptcy court. All debts and all assets must be disclosed. One cannot pick and choose between creditors; all must be disclosed to the court. Failure to do so can result in a denial of bankruptcy "discharge," which will leave you and your assets vulnerable to attack by your creditors.

5. Bankruptcy is a privilege under federal law, as provided for in the U.S. Constitution. It is intended to offer a debtor a "fresh start," provided the debtor has conducted his or her affairs honestly.

"How Did I Get to This Point?"
Almost every individual who files for bankruptcy asks the question: "How did I get to this point?" The question is part of a universal feeling among those experiencing bankruptcy for the first time that they are alone, although millions of their fellow citizens have reached the same situation they now face.

When It's Time to Face the Facts

We have all heard or read about the big corporations, movie stars, and millionaire wheeler-dealers who file for bankruptcy. Many people do not realize that hundreds of thousands of Americans just like themselves turn to the protection of the bankruptcy laws each year.

The first thing to understand about people who file bankruptcy is that they are as different from each other as is the general population. They come in all sizes, colors, religions, ages, and socioeconomic levels. No particular group produces more bankruptcy filings, on average, than any other group. Bankruptcy filers include individuals from some of the wealthiest families and from the poorest. They include housewives, lawyers, day laborers, doctors, and farmers. They are, or were, unemployed, employed, or self-employed. People in all professions, no matter how high or low, are susceptible to bankruptcy.

Although there are no "typical" debtors who file bankruptcy, in a statistical sense, many have experienced losses or disappointments that helped lead them into a debt situation from which bankruptcy appeared to be the only escape.

Three Profiles in Bankruptcy

The following cases represent, as much as possible, a cross section of the people who file bankruptcy. They are taken from recent studies of bankruptcy filings. Only the names and clearly identifying details have been changed to protect the privacy of the people involved.

Although these examples include only a few of the reasons individuals and couples face bankruptcy, they do convey the types of situations that are at the root of many bankruptcy filings.

After moving three times in seven years, Paul and Susan Britton ended up in northern Ohio where Paul was employed as an unskilled construction worker. At the time of their bankruptcy filing, which was in 1987, Paul was employed by

You *Can* Go Bankrupt *Without* Going Broke

the same contracting company for eight months. During the previous two years his earnings were $27,000 and $29,000, respectively. Mrs. Britton worked as a receptionist at a dental clinic for eighteen months. Her income was $22,000 a year.

When they filed bankruptcy, the Brittons rented a small house and owned a seven-year-old Buick they had purchased used. They both used the Buick for transportation to and from their jobs. They had no cash and no savings and reported that their personal and household possessions were worth about $800.

Paul and Susan Brittons' bankruptcy filing showed they had accumulated $24,635 worth of debts. Of this, $3,410 was a secured debt to a furniture store, and the remaining $21,225 was in fourteen unsecured debts.

The Brittons' dischargeable debts were

St. Helen's Hospital	$3,650
Ohio Personal Finance	3,087
South Coast Clinic	2,319
Dr. Rosencranz	2,000
Northside Hospital	1,950
Dr. Loomis	1,600
J.C. Penney Company	1,585
Central City Clinic	1,550
Dr. Goodwin	1,527
Dr. Thresher	525
Northern Ohio Telephone	387
Public Service Gas & Electric	350
Midwest Laboratories	320
West Street Pharmacy	200
Sears, Roebuck and Company	175

Although we don't know exactly why Paul and Susan Britton became so deeply in debt, there are certain assumptions we can make based on those debts.

When It's Time to Face the Facts

Most of the debts were incurred three to four years before their bankruptcy filing. This leads us to believe they had struggled for several years to pay their debts before the filing. The small size of many of the debts indicates they may have paid substantial payments to their creditors during those years. When this is combined with the insignificant value of their possessions, it is safe to say the Brittons were not typical "deadbeats" who ran up large debts they did not plan on repaying for luxury or other expensive items.

The unusual number of medical-related bills from hospitals, doctors, and clinics were the result of a series of illnesses suffered by both Paul and Susan. There is also the possibility they changed doctors regularly because they couldn't pay the bills.

While there are many factors that help drive people into bankruptcy, by far the biggest and most influential is the general addiction to consumer credit. Our apparently unquenchable thirst for easy credit has now become a major force driving the nation's economy. According to the Federal Reserve, consumer debt was $307.2 billion at the end of 1980. A decade later it had more than doubled to $736.7 billion. Most frightening, the biggest increase in all consumer debt was in the costliest, the high-interest credit cards. During that same decade the credit card portion of debt jumped from 18 to 29 percent of the total. The human cost of the credit card life-style so many people live began to take its toll during 1990. The percentage of delinquent credit card accounts rose by 16 percent from the second to the third quarters alone.

While we hear a lot about drug addiction, alcohol addiction, and even gambling addiction, little attention is paid to what may be the most devastating addiction of all, credit addiction. So many Americans are addicted to the use of credit that their habit has spawned billion-dollar industries providing credit to consumers, keeping and selling information on people's credit status, and funding the companies that issue credit cards; therefore, it is simply bad business for many to speak out on credit addiction.

A good example of what credit addiction can do to otherwise normal people is the fate of William and Nina Martin. William, 38, worked as a middle-level manager for a major international corporation with headquarters in New York City. His $86,000 annual salary provided a comfortable life for the couple and their two children. They lived in an upper-middle-class town in western Connecticut. William drove his two-year-old Buick to the Stamford railroad station each day for the trip into New York, and Nina ran her errands in a three-year-old Mazda.

Inside the Martins' attractive and manicured colonial home, the furniture was new, as was their clothing. They seemed to be living the American dream, when suddenly it all fell apart. Almost everything the Martins owned was bought on credit, usually with high-interest credit cards. Their debt was almost $45,000, not including the mortgage on their home, when the first serious sign of trouble arrived. It was a threat from a creditor to place a garnishee against William's salary. Until then the Martins had been managing to get from month to month by performing an incredible balancing act of deciding which creditors to pay and which to hold at bay. They knew they were headed for trouble, but both refused to face the reality. The Martins had become, like so many others in debt, dreamers filled with the hope that somehow someday, if they could keep balancing their monthly payments, something would happen to get them out of their mess. It didn't.

In an effort to stave off their creditors the Martins have sought the advice of an attorney. They now face the possibility of having to file for bankruptcy, which, because they live in a state with no homestead exemption law that might protect them from losing their home, might end up costing them their house.

The other addictions, drugs, alcohol, and gambling, are also major factors that contribute to financial problems leading to bankruptcy. A typical case is that of Ellen Dobson.

At age 26, Ellen described her life as having "never been normal." Caught up in the fast-paced singles life, she quickly found herself addicted to both drugs and alcohol. During the first few years after moving out of her parent's home and into her own apartment she was able to maintain a good office job and still lead a "fast and high" social life. Eventually it began to catch up with her, causing an unusually high number of absences from work and even situations of erratic behavior that cost her the job she held for three years. Despondent over the loss of her job, Ellen increasingly turned to drugs and alcohol to lift her spirits. Because of her behavior, she was unable to keep another steady job and soon tried her hand at working as an office temp. Although there was work available, it was never quite enough to pay her bills, so she started to rely on her credit cards and the overdraft privileges of her checking account to pay some of her bills, and of course to help her maintain the life-style to which she was addicted. Soon she was paying over $1,500 a month just to meet the minimum payments on her accounts.

Changing jobs, fluctuating salaries, and the constantly increasing costs of maintaining her drug and alcohol addictions contributed further to her complete loss of control over her life. She was living way beyond her means and was totally out of control. She recognized the direness of her condition but was ashamed to admit what she saw as her failures, and was too embarrassed to seek help. To make matters worse, the drug and alcohol abuse made her physically ill, which led to even more absences from any jobs she could find. All this was compounded by the fear that her creditors, who were not yet aware of her situation because she was still managing to pay her monthly bills, would eventually garnish her salary, take back her automobile, and generally make her life even more miserable.

Finally, Ellen found the strength to ask for help. She turned to a friend who convinced her to see an attorney the friend knew who specialized in handling financial problems. "I walked into his office like a lost puppy, needing understanding, direction, and guidance." Ellen was lucky that she found someone who was able to give her those things she needed. Feeling that everything she had worked for was destroyed, Ellen listened as the attorney explained her rights under the bankruptcy laws. The attorney realized Ellen was in a bad situation that was rapidly becoming worse. He recommended she file a Chapter 7 bankruptcy case, which would enable her to start over again financially and allow her the time and peace of mind to deal with her drug and alcohol problems.

Today, one year after filing her bankruptcy petition, Ellen is no longer addicted to drugs or alcohol. She has a steady job with a large company and is working hard to rebuild her former good credit standing. Did the bankruptcy help? Ellen can answer that in her own words: "I went through Chapter 7 bankruptcy and am glad I did. My life is now free of the awful stress and depression my debts had gotten me into."

Many people in many different circumstances turn to bankruptcy. They now number nearly one million per year. A great many others fail to recognize that bankruptcy may be the only realistic way to solve their financial dilemma and continue trying to keep paying for credit they should have never used in the first place.

Two

DEBTORS HAVE RIGHTS, KNOW YOURS

The law protects you as a debtor in the same way it protects all citizens. The actions your creditors are permitted to take against you are clearly defined by federal and state laws that are intended to prevent creditors from abusing you and your rights. The most important thing you must do as a debtor is to understand what your rights are, what actions creditors can and cannot take against you, what you can do to stop illegal actions by a creditor, and what remedies are available to you under the law.

What can you do when a creditor sends you a dunning letter or calls on the telephone threatening to take you to court? How do you handle harassing telephone calls from creditors or collection agencies while you are at work?

A vital bit of information every debtor should know is that most communications between a debtor and creditor, or a creditor's representative, such as a collection agency, are regulated by law. In this chapter we'll review these laws, explain how they might apply to your situation, and demonstrate how you can best use them to your advantage. Where appropriate, we've included sample letters and other items you may wish to use when communicating with creditors and debt collectors.

We will also describe how a credit bureau works, explain what your rights are when dealing with the Internal Revenue Service, show you what actions you can take that will get debt collectors off your back, and tell you what to do when a creditor threatens you with criminal prosecution.

CONSUMER PROTECTION LAWS

First, we will examine the federal laws dealing with consumer relations regarding creditors. These are

- The Truth in Lending Act
- The Equal Credit Opportunity Act
- The Fair Credit Billing Act
- The Fair Credit Reporting Act
- The Fair Debt Collection Practices Act

The key words in the titles of these federal laws are "Truth," "Equal," and "Fair." These laws are designed to protect consumers from unscrupulous lenders, error-prone record keeping by consumer credit reporting agencies, and unprincipled debt collection companies.

The Truth in Lending Act

This is a disclosure law that requires a lender to state plainly the terms of an installment loan contract in language which is concise and uniform. Credit customers have the right to sue a lender who fails to comply with the law. It also provides a three-day waiting period on loan applications when a home is used as collateral, such as a home improvement loan or a home equity loan. During this waiting period, the consumer can cancel the transaction without penalty.

Debtors Have Rights, Know Yours

The act requires lenders to tell each customer the annual percentage rate for a loan as determined by a national uniform system known as the "actuarial method." The lender is further required to tell the customer exactly how much the loan will cost in dollars and cents, including all charges for interest, fees, and insurance and any other charges accruing in the transaction.

The following is a sample letter you can use to cancel a loan when your home is used as collateral for a home improvement loan.

Mr. William Constable
Topflight Home Improvement Company
2121 Oak Street
Anytown, Anystate 12345

Dear Mr. Constable:
This is to inform you that I wish to cancel our agreement of (date) to add vinyl siding to my home at the above address. Since we made the agreement last evening, I have changed my mind and decided to wait until next spring to have the work done. Please return my down payment as soon as possible.
I appreciate your help and will contact you when I decide to go ahead with the job.

Sincerely,

Under the law the contractor has ten days in which to return the down payment. If you send the letter registered or certified mail and imply as this one does that the contractor may still get the job, you might avoid the delaying tactics some contractors use to hold your money as long as they can.

The Equal Credit Opportunity Act
This law is intended to prevent creditors from using an applicant's age, religion, race, sex, marital status, national

origin, or the fact the applicant receives public assistance as a reason to deny credit. Except for marital status, credit applications can no longer ask questions about any of these subjects. An applicant's marital status can be a proper subject for a credit application if the applicant lives in a community property state or relies on property located in a community property state for repayment of the loan, or if the application is made for a joint account or is a secured account.

The Fair Credit Billing Act

This law protects you against unfair and inaccurate billing practices. It was intended to apply specifically to transactions known as "open-end" accounts, such as department store revolving charge accounts and credit cards. In both cases the consumer receives a monthly statement which might contain errors or unfair charges.

If your statement or bill contains a charge for something you did not purchase, or has the wrong price for an item you did purchase, or includes an item you returned or of which you refused delivery or a charge you can't understand, or contains a mistake in arithmetic, you can invoke your rights under this law. Specific instructions for doing this are given under the subheading "How to Resolve Billing Disputes" later in this chapter.

The Fair Credit Reporting Act

This law is designed to protect consumers against the dissemination by consumer reporting agencies of obsolete or erroneous information. The law requires that any company refusing to grant you credit based in whole or in part on the information in a credit report obtained from a credit reporting agency inform you of that fact and the name and address of the agency issuing the credit report.

Debtors Have Rights, Know Yours

It also entitles you to have inaccurate, obsolete, or incomplete information removed from your credit file. This is not as simple as it may sound, since you have to track down every credit reporting agency which has a file on you and challenge the incorrect information in your file. For specific instructions on your rights under this law, see the following discussions in this chapter: "What to Do If You Are Refused Credit" and "How to Check Your Credit File."

The Fair Debt Collection Practices Act

This law regulates the activities of debt collectors, prohibiting certain practices entirely. The law covers debts incurred for the purchase of a car, for medical care, and for charge accounts.

A debt collector is any person, other than the creditor, who regularly collects debts owed to third parties. This includes attorneys who collect debts on a regular basis.

A debt collector can legally contact you in person or by telephone, mail, or telegram. You may not, however, be contacted at inconvenient or unusual times or places. For example, a debt collector violates this federal law if an attempt is made to speak to you during your daughter's christening or your son's Bar Mitzvah, or if you are contacted in the middle of the night, unless you gave prior approval.

Many people who are in debt fear the ramifications which might arise if their employer learns of their situation. Fortunately, the law bans a debt collector from contacting you at work if the debt collector has reason to believe your employer disapproves. The best way to be sure the debt collector knows your boss's attitude is to write the collection agency a letter, using "return receipt requested" postage stating that its employees cannot contact you at your place of employment.

You will find additional information on what to do about

debt collectors who harass you under the heading "Dealing with Debt Collectors," later in this chapter.

CONSUMER REPORTING AGENCIES AND YOUR CREDIT FILE

Sometimes called credit bureaus or credit agencies, these are private companies which operate for a profit. They have no connection with any government agency. The use of the words "agency" and "bureau" is misleading and unfortunate because they give many people the impression these companies have official government standing. They do not, and their business practices are regulated by numerous federal and state laws.

Consumer reporting agencies are companies that collect, store, and sell information about you and millions of other consumers. The five major consumer reporting agencies are TRW Credit, Trans Union Credit, Credit Bureau, Inc. Equifax, Associated Credit, and Chilton Corp. Each company has offices in dozens of states. If you have been using credit cards, or any other type of credit, it is likely each of these five, and most of the other smaller companies, has a file containing information on you.

Although these companies are supposed to keep your file current and accurate, errors regularly creep into millions of consumer credit files each year. According to Texas Assistant Attorney General Stephen Gardner, "The whole credit system is out of control. Not only are your financial matters virtually an open book, but it's an open book with a couple of pages missing, some lines crossed out, and some pieces in backward."

The accuracy and timeliness of your file is vitally important, because every time you apply for credit of any kind, from a charge account at a local store to a home mortgage,

Debtors Have Rights, Know Yours

one of the first steps a potential lender or creditor does on receiving your application is to obtain a copy of your credit report.

What's in Your Credit File

The information contained in your credit file will be used by the potential creditor to help determine whether you are likely to repay the loan or pay your monthly bills in a timely fashion. Often it is the sole determining factor on which the decision about your creditworthiness is based. Obviously it is important that you know what information about you these companies have in their files and that you take steps to correct any errors or obsolete information.

Your credit file contains information about you which can be divided into these five categories:

1. *Identifying.* This is information which identifies who you are, such as your name, address, and social security number.
2. *Employment.* This includes the name and address of your employer, the position you hold, how long you have worked there, previous employers, and your current income.
3. *Personal.* This is a brief biographical sketch that tells a potential creditor or employer your date of birth, the number of dependents you have, your previous addresses, and information about your previous employment history.
4. *Credit History.* This category contains information about your previous experience with credit, including what accounts you currently have, what accounts you had in the past, if you paid your bills on time, if you had serious disputes with previous creditors, and if you defaulted on loans.
5. *Public Information.* These are data that are available to

anyone who has the time and patience to learn what they can about you from public records such as courthouse and county clerk records. This includes records of tax liens, death, marriage, divorce, bankruptcies, and court judgments.

As you can see, your credit file contains a lot of information about you which can be extremely damaging if it is inaccurate or obsolete.

How does this information get in your file and what do these companies do with it? The agencies that collect and sell the data in your credit files make no attempt to rate or evaluate your creditworthiness. Only the credit analyst at the bank or company from which you request credit does that. When you apply for credit, miss a payment on a charge account, default on a loan, or do anything else which relates to your credit profile, it is usually reported to one or more of the companies previously listed. The credit bureau does not verify the validity of the information sent to it by its subscribers. It simply includes that information in your file, even if it is inaccurate.

Eventually the credit bureau will sell that information to an interested party who for some reason is checking on your credit rating. The credit bureau is constrained by law to sell that information only to a legitimate party who it believes will use the information exclusively for certain clearly defined purposes. These are:

1. To grant you credit, review your account, or collect on your account.
2. To consider you for possible employment or promotion.
3. To evaluate the underwriting of insurance for which you have applied.
4. To decide if you are eligible for a license or other benefit

granted by some agency of government which is required by law to consider your financial responsibility or status.
5. To comply with a court order.
6. To fulfill a request in connection with a business transaction between you and another person, as long as the person requesting the report has a legitimate business need for the report.
7. To disclose credit information to anyone to whom you have given written permission for such disclosure.
8. To provide identifying information to a governmental agency.

The information in your credit file is available to a wide range of people, companies, and governmental agencies. It is imperative that it contain no incorrect or obsolete information which can cause you harm.

How to Check Your Credit File

Federal consumer protection laws recognize the impact credit files have on a person's life. Because of this, there are clear guidelines which grant you the right to know what information credit bureaus have in your file and what steps you can take to correct errors or remove incomplete or obsolete information.

There are two ways in which you can legally review the information in your credit file. The first is to invoke your right to know what is in your file. The law does not give you the right to see or even hold your actual file, but you are entitled to know the "nature and substance" of the information in your file.

First, look for the local offices of each credit bureau. These can be found in the Yellow Pages of your telephone directory under the heading "Credit Reporting Agencies." There may be several listed in your directory. You can call, write, or visit each of them to find out if they have a file on you.

If you elect to write, include your name, current address, telephone number, and social security number in your correspondence. If you attempt to get the information over the telephone, you may find the credit agency will ask you to write or provide evidence that you are who you say you are. If you decide to visit the agency, it is advisable to call ahead for an appointment or at least determine during what hours appropriate records will be available. You can bring one other person, such as an attorney, to review the information with you. Be sure you both have acceptable proof of identification with you. Be prepared to pay a fee for the privilege of reviewing the information in your file. The law allows credit agencies to charge a nominal fee for this service.

The second way of getting a look at the information in your file will not cost you a thing, but it applies only if you have been refused credit. The law gives you the right to see the information in any credit report that was provided to a creditor or insurance issuer if you were refused credit or insurance, or forced to pay higher interest or premium rates because of the information in that file. For detailed instructions, refer to the section "What to Do If You Are Refused Credit."

Credit agencies handle millions of pieces of information about millions of people each year. They are not infallible. They frequently make mistakes. The most common errors appearing in consumer credit files are

1. A current account is reported as past due even though you have never been late in making a scheduled payment.
2. Debts belonging to someone else are reported as being yours.

Debtors Have Rights, Know Yours

3. Payment for merchandise you returned or for which you refused delivery is reported as an unpaid debt in spite of the fact the company from which you purchased the merchandise from issued you a full credit.
4. Old accounts which were paid in full years ago remain in the file with open unpaid balances.
5. Computer errors or mathematical errors show incorrect balances.
6. Information has been coded incorrectly by a credit agency employee, thus showing some data as negative when it really is not.
7. Obsolete information is included in your file.

Any information that you believe is incorrect or incomplete may be challenged. Complete instructions for doing this appear under the subheading "How to Correct Your Credit File."

What to Do If You Are Refused Credit

If you are refused credit or insurance because of information provided by a credit agency, you are entitled to see that information at no charge if you request it within thirty days of notification to you of the refusal. If you were denied employment because of information in a credit bureau file, you have sixty days to request the right to review that information.

To simplify our description of the process, we will refer to a refusal of credit, but the process is the same for the others mentioned. The letter you receive from a creditor advising you that your application has been denied must tell you if the decision was based on information in your credit bureau file. The letter will also contain a reference number and the name and address of the credit agency which provided the report.

You *Can* Go Bankrupt *Without* Going Broke

When you receive this letter you should write to the credit agency requesting a copy of the report. In your letter include the name and address of the company which refused your application and the reference number in the creditor's letter. It is also advisable to enclose a photocopy (not the original) of the letter from the creditor rejecting your credit application.

Here is a sample letter which may be used for this purpose:

Your State Credit Bureau
1234 Central Avenue
Your City and State 12345

Reference No. 123456789012

I was recently refused credit by the ABC Company of Your City based on a credit report supplied by your agency. I would like to find out what information is in my credit file and therefore request that you send me a copy of my credit report as quickly as possible.

I am enclosing a copy of the letter I received from ABC Company for identification purposes.

Sincerely,

Send the letter "return receipt requested" so that you will have clear Postal Service evidence that it was received by the credit agency.

You should receive a copy of your credit report in two to three weeks. If you do not receive it after twenty days, send a follow-up letter before the thirty-day request period expires.

How to Correct Your Credit File

If, when you receive the report, it contains incorrect information, you can request the credit agency to investigate your

Debtors Have Rights, Know Yours

claim. Unless it has substantial reason to believe your claim is frivolous or irrelevant, the credit agency is required to investigate it. If it determines the original information was wrong, it is required to correct the file to reflect the new information. You are then entitled to a list of everyone to whom the agency supplied a copy of your credit report in the past six months. You may then require the agency to advise all of them of the corrections in your file.

If a credit agency fails to comply, it can be subject to fines and criminal penalties. You can also sue the agency for damages.

Following is a sample of the type of information to include in a letter to a credit agency requesting an investigation of information contained in a credit file:

> On reviewing a copy of my credit report supplied by your agency I found one item of information which I believe is incorrect. I would like you to investigate and correct it.
>
> The item is my account with XYZ Company. According to the file, XYZ Company reported that my account was delinquent and was referred to a collection agency for payment. This is not correct. I have always paid that account on a timely basis and have never been notified that I was delinquent or that the account was turned over to a collection agency. I would appreciate your correcting this inaccurate information as quickly as possible.

If after investigating your claim the agency notifies you, as it is required by law, that it will not remove or change the information, you can file a statement of dispute which becomes a part of your file. Usually limited to no more than one hundred words, the statement of dispute must then be included with your credit report whenever a report is requested by anyone. For example, suppose the agency investigated the claim in the preceding letter, but for some reason failed or refused to correct the file. The following example is the consumer's statement of dispute in response to that failure.

> I do not believe my payment record with the XYZ Company is listed correctly. I usually pay my bills as soon as I receive them (but never later than two weeks after they come). The information in my credit file stating that my account with XYZ Company was overdue and had been sent to a collection agency is incorrect. I was never sent a single overdue notice, was never contacted by a collection agency, and was always paid up on this account. I think the problem is the result of a clerical error and should have been corrected long ago.

The statement of dispute should express your position clearly and concisely. Explain and present the facts in simple language so a potential creditor can understand precisely what you are saying. Two things the statement must do if it is to work in your favor are clearly identify the information in your file which you contend is incorrect and incomplete, and explain why.

Except where large sums of money are involved ($50,000 or more), information in a consumer's credit file eventually becomes obsolete and cannot be included in most credit reports. Most adverse information must be deleted after seven years. The only adverse information which can be included for a longer period is a bankruptcy. A Chapter 7 bankruptcy may remain in your file for a maximum of ten years; a Chapter 13 filing must be expunged after seven years.

How to Resolve Billing Disputes

Assume you purchased a television at a department store and

Debtors Have Rights, Know Yours

charged the total amount of the sale. When you receive the charge account statement listing the purchase, the amount is larger than the price you agreed to pay. What do you do?

Under the rules of the Fair Credit Billing Act you have the right to challenge the charge and demand that the retailer or the bank issuing the credit card promptly rectify the error.

The law defines a billing error as any charge

- not made by you or someone you authorized to use your account
- poorly identified, for a different amount or on a different date from that shown on the statement
- made for something you did not accept on delivery or that was not delivered according to agreement

Billing errors can also include

- failure to issue a credit to your account in the correct amount or in a timely manner
- accounting, mathematical, or computer mistakes
- failure to mail your statement to your current address provided you notified the creditor of your new address in writing at least twenty days before the billing period ended
- a request for additional information or an explanation concerning a questionable item for which you were charged

If any of these situations apply to you, you can ask the creditor to correct your account.

Use the address on the billing statement to notify the creditor of the error. You have sixty days from the date the bill was mailed to make this notification. Don't waste time and money calling the creditor on the telephone, as a phone call will not protect your rights under the law. Send the letter "return receipt requested" so you have a signed statement that the letter was received and keep a copy of the actual letter for your records. Be sure to include the following information in your letter: your name and account number, a statement that you believe there is an error, an explanation of why you believe there is an error, and the amount of the error.

Following is a sample of a consumer's letter informing a creditor of a billing error:

> Accounts Division
> Universal Credit Card Company
> Box 567
> Any Town, Any State 12345
>
> I am writing to inform you that a statement you sent me dated October 24, 1991, contains a billing error in the amount of $12.54. The watch I bought using my Universal credit card had a total cost of $67.89, but on my bill the cost is listed as $79.43. I would appreciate it if you would correct the mistake. My account number is 123-456-789.

The creditor must acknowledge your letter within thirty days and must correct your account or give you an explanation of why the creditor believes the bill is correct.

DEALING WITH DEBT COLLECTORS

There was a time when debt collectors were notorious for hounding debtors at their homes, jobs, and anywhere else they could be located. It was not uncommon for a debt collector to call a debtor's boss and tell him or her all about the debtor's financial irresponsibility. Under the law debt collectors can no longer do this.

Debt collectors' practices are now tightly regulated by

Debtors Have Rights, Know Yours

federal law. A debt collector (anyone who regularly collects debts owed to others) may no longer engage in harassing tactics to collect debts. A debt collector who does so may be subject to arrest for assault or sued for libel, slander, or even invasion of privacy.

What Debt Collectors Can Do

A debt collector may contact you by mail, telephone, telegram, or in person. A collector may contact other people who know you, but only to find out where you live or work. Within five days of the initial contact by a debt collector, the collector must send you written notice telling you how much money you owe, the name of the creditor to whom you owe the money, and what you can do if you believe you do not owe the debt.

What Debt Collectors Can't Do

A debt collector cannot tell any other person about your debt, including your employer, friends, or relatives. The only person other than you with whom the debt collector may discuss this information is your attorney, provided you have informed the debt collector of your attorney's name, address, and telephone number.

If you owe debts to several creditors who are represented by the same debt collector, any payment you make must be applied to the debt you specify. The debt collector cannot apply it to any other debt.

Following is a list of actions debt collectors are not permitted to take.

Debt collectors cannot legally

- use threats of violence or harm to you, your property, or reputation
- publish or otherwise make public your name as a consumer who refuses to pay your debts

- use obscene or profane language
- repeatedly use the telephone to annoy someone
- fail to identify themselves when telephoning
- falsely imply they are an attorney or a government representative
- falsely imply you have committed a crime
- misrepresent the amount you owe
- claim papers being sent are legal documents when they aren't
- indicate papers being sent are not legal documents when they are
- give false credit information about you to anyone
- send you anything that looks like an official court or government document which is not
- use a false name
- say you will be arrested if you don't pay your debt (debt is a civil matter, not a criminal one)
- threaten to take action against you, your property, or your salary which they are not permitted to do under the law
- collect an amount larger than what you owe
- deposit your postdated payment check before the date on the check
- make you accept collect calls or pay for telegrams
- contact you by postcard

What Debtors Can Do

You can stop a debt collector from contacting you for up to thirty days by sending the collection agency a letter claiming you do not owe the money. The agency is then obligated to investigate your claim. If it finds proof of your debt, such as a signed bill, it must provide you with a copy of that proof. Only then is it free to resume contacting you for payment.

A debtor can stop a debt collector from any form of

contact simply by writing a letter to the collection agency asking it to stop. Once the collection agency receives your letter, it may no longer contact you except to tell you there will be no future contacts or to advise you it is taking some specific action, provided it is actually taking that action.

If you believe a debt collector has violated the laws governing such activities, you can report the collection agency to your state attorney general's office or to the Federal Trade Commission. You may also be able to sue the debt collection agency in a state or federal court. If you win, you may recover money for damages you suffered, as well as court and attorney costs.

If a debt collector engages in activities you believe are illegal, contact an attorney who specializes in such matters. The attorney will not only be able to protect your rights, but the mere presence of an attorney will have a calming effect on a debt collector who has gotten out of hand.

Never allow a creditor or a debt collector to rattle you. If you receive a call from a debt collector threatening to have you imprisoned, don't panic. *You cannot be put in prison for failing to pay a debt.* Inform the caller that you are fully aware of your rights under federal and state law and that any further threats of criminal action will be reported to the appropriate federal and state agencies. When the debt collector and/or the creditor realize you know your legal rights, they are both apt to act in a more lawful manner and refrain from threatening or harassing you.

One training seminar for debt collectors instructs them to take charge of a conversation with a debtor by not talking the most but by asking the most questions. The instructor counsels his group, "Ask the debtor what he can tell you about his account; then shut up. Six seconds will sound like an eternity to him."

The trick here is to get you to start talking, perhaps feel

guilty about not repaying your debt, and even offer to pay at least something to ease your conscience. The most effective response to this ploy is to put the ball in the other court. Tell the collector you don't recall; can the collector tell you about it? Then stop talking. Allow the silence to hang. Do not be the first to speak!

In many respects debt collectors are like salespeople trying to convince you to do what they want you to do. There's an old saying among salespeople that you state your case why the customer should buy from you, then you stop talking and wait, the theory being that "the first one to talk loses." The meaning of that is that the first person to talk, the salesperson or the customer, is placed at a disadvantage by speaking. Don't let a debt collector do that to you. Remain silent—let the debt collector do the talking. Nothing is more frustrating to a debt collector than dealing with a creditor who refuses to be drawn into a lengthy conversation and who simply "acts dumb."

DEALING WITH THE INTERNAL REVENUE SERVICE

The one government agency Americans are loath to deal with is the Internal Revenue Service. The IRS is charged with collecting federal taxes, auditing the returns of individuals and businesses, and charging penalties to those it finds guilty of cheating on their taxes or those who have underpaid their taxes through an error. The penalties can sometimes be as crippling as the tax bill itself. Perhaps the most well-publicized tax penalty was the $5,000 per day charged to country singer Willie Nelson.

People confronted with accusations or actions by IRS employees usually feel they are dealing with an autonomous government agency having unlimited power, and in many respects they are right. The Internal Revenue Service is one of the most powerful government entities, and it frequently appears to trample on citizens' rights.

Even Congress recognized there was legitimate cause to fear some of the high-handed tactics employed by the IRS. In a rare move to protect citizens from illegal activities by IRS representatives, Congress passed landmark legislation in 1988, creating what has become known as "The Taxpayer Bill of Rights." This law requires the Internal Revenue Service to give a simple, nontechnical disclosure statement to any taxpayer it contacts about a tax determination or collection of taxes.

The Taxpayer Bill of Rights
The disclosure statement the IRS must distribute advises taxpayers of

1. the rights of a taxpayer and the obligations of the IRS during an audit
2. the procedures by which a taxpayer can appeal an adverse IRS decision, both administratively and judicially
3. the procedures for processing refund claims and filing taxpayer complaints
4. the procedures the IRS can legally use to enforce tax laws, including seizure of property and the filing of liens against property.

Although still more powerful than most taxpayers are comfortable with, the IRS can no longer run rampant over citizens rights. In a momentary flush of bravery, Congress took steps to protect citizens from the IRS by placing limits on the actions of its agents and representatives.

What the IRS Must Do

The IRS cannot record an interview with a taxpayer by taping the interview, using a stenographer, or even handwritten note taking unless it has met certain conditions, including giving the taxpayer advance notice. A copy of the transcript or recording must be given the taxpayer on request, at the taxpayer's expense.

The IRS must suspend an interview at any time if the taxpayer being interviewed clearly states the desire to consult an attorney, certified public accountant, or any other person permitted to represent a taxpayer before the IRS. Exempted from this rule are certain interviews that are initiated by an administrative summons.

A taxpayer cannot be required to attend an interview if the taxpayer is represented by an attorney or other acceptable person with written power of attorney, unless an administrative summons has been issued. The IRS can however, notify a taxpayer that a legally constituted representative is causing unreasonable delay or hindrance of the examination.

The IRS cannot impose a penalty or addition to tax if it is due to erroneous written advice furnished by an IRS office or employee in response to a taxpayer's specific written request. For obvious reasons this is a hard rule of which to take advantage, because the taxpayer must prove he or she reasonably relied on the advice and furnished adequate and accurate information on which the advice was based.

Perhaps most important of all, the Internal Revenue Service is prohibited from imposing production quotas on agents or supervisors based on how much money they collect from taxpayers. They are also prohibited from evaluating these employees based on the same criteria.

What a Taxpayer Can Do

If you are interviewed by the IRS you can make an audio recording of the interview if you give the IRS advance notice, pay for the recording yourself, and use your own equipment.

You are entitled to representation, and as we already said, we strongly urge you to take advantage of this right. Your representative can appear on your behalf, except in a criminal investigation where you are also required to attend.

You can insist that audits be conducted at the IRS office nearest to where you live and require that the audit be transferred if you change your place of residence.

You can request a change in the time set for an audit or interview. The time must be mutually agreed on between you and the IRS.

If you can prove that immediate action by the IRS will cause you significant hardship, you can apply to the Problem Resolution Office for relief. Your application can be made in writing, orally, or by completing IRS Form 911. The Problem Resolution Office has the power to halt collection actions temporarily pending an investigation of your hardship claim.

There are many other restrictions placed on the IRS by the 1988 law dealing with its treatment of liens, property seizures, and so on. The most important point to remember when dealing with the IRS is to be adequately represented by someone fully familiar with the tax laws and the procedures and practices of the Internal Revenue Service. Without that representation you may place yourself at a serious disadvantage.

ALWAYS BE PROTECTED AND PREPARED

Never deal with creditors, debt collection agencies, credit bureaus, or the Internal Revenue Service unprotected or unprepared. Being prepared means being aware of your rights. All your communications with these people are regulated by law, but there are so many laws and administrative regulations that it is virtually impossible for the average person to know them all. Being protected means seeking advice from an expert in these matters. Too often people who try to use the do-it-yourself approach to financial-legal matters suffer the consequence of using amateur advice. Attorneys, accountants, tax practitioners, and others work with these laws every day. The advice of one of these experts could save you money and heartache.

UPDATE

As we go to press the credit reporting company, TRW, has announced that it will provide, to every consumer who requests it, a copy of his or her credit report once each year at no charge. This change in policy came in the midst of Congressional hearings focusing on the practices and policies of these companies, following disclosure that TRW had erroneously recorded in the files of 1,500 residents of Norwich, Vermont that there were tax liens against their homes. Other credit reporting companies are expected to follow TRW's lead.

Three

FINDING ALTERNATIVES TO BANKRUPTCY

Personal bankruptcy may be the only solution for some financial problems, but too frequently people contemplating bankruptcy fail to consider or even realize that other alternatives are available. This chapter will present some of those alternatives and help you determine if your specific situation can be resolved through one of them. We will also discuss where you should and should not seek help in making this decision.

WHEN BANKRUPTCY WILL NOT WORK

In many situations bankruptcy is not only a poor alternative, but it may not even be a viable option. Before considering alternatives to bankruptcy, let's look at some situations where bankruptcy is absolutely the wrong avenue for a debtor to seek relief.

If Your Debts Are Secured

Bankruptcy releases a debtor from the responsibility of repaying unsecured debts and possibly certain secured debts.

You *Can* Go Bankrupt *Without* Going Broke

Secured debts are those for which you pledged something of value, such as a home, a car, or furniture or jewelry. Bankruptcy Chapters 7 and 13 (and in certain circumstances Chapters 11 and 12) offer a debtor the possibility of retaining certain property that was used to secure a loan. An example of this is a loan used to purchase a car. If when you file for bankruptcy you have not yet repaid your auto loan, and the lender holds a lien against the car, you can satisfy the lien by paying your creditor the book value of the car even if that is less than the amount owed. If the actual value of the car is less than the amount owing, the balance may be treated as any other unsecured debt.

> When Elizabeth Preston filed a Chapter 7 bankruptcy petition, she owed $11,000 to the bank where she obtained her auto loan. The book value of the car was now only $8,500. Elizabeth wanted to keep the car, and she was able to borrow enough money from relatives to pay the bank the value of the car, $8,500. The remaining $2,500 was treated as an unsecured loan and discharged along with Elizabeth's other unsecured debts.

Had Elizabeth filed a Chapter 13 bankruptcy case she might have been able to reduce her monthly car loan payments, stretch them out over a longer time, and still pay only the value of the car at the time of her bankruptcy. In other words, $2,500 of her $11,000 debt to the bank would have been treated as an unsecured loan.

The single secured debt lender treated differently is the mortgage holder on a home. Mortgage lenders are given preferred status in a bankruptcy. With rare exceptions, debtors filing for bankruptcy face the prospect of losing their home just as they would under any circumstance where they fail to make their payments. In certain situations, a Chapter

Finding Alternatives To Bankruptcy

13 (or sometimes a Chapter 11 or 12) bankruptcy may permit a homeowner who has fallen behind in mortgage payments to develop a plan to make up missed payments and penalties over a period of time, providing all current and future payments are made on time.

Even if you are able to make timely monthly mortgage payments, your home may not be completely free from attachment by creditors, including unsecured creditors. Most states permit a person filing bankruptcy to retain at least some portion of home ownership. This varies widely from state to state. For a guide to these exemptions by state, see Chapter 11.

As a general rule under state law, creditors can ask the court to sell your home to satisfy your debts if the value of the home is more than the combined total of the outstanding mortgage and the state homestead exemption.

For example, let's assume you live in a state which permits a $10,000 exemption of equity in your home against repayment of your debts. The current market value of the home is $60,000, and you owe $51,500 on your mortgage. Because the equity ownership of the house is $9,500, and this amount is less than the state exemption law of $10,000, creditors cannot force the sale of the house. If you are able to keep your mortgage payments current, the mortgage lender will have no interest in acting against you.

But, if the present value of the house is $80,000, then even unsecured creditors can request that your house be sold to satisfy the debts. In that case if the house is sold for $80,000, the mortgage lender will receive $51,500 as repayment for the mortgage, you will receive $10,000 as your exempt portion under the law, and the remaining $18,500 will be used to satisfy your debts.

If the amount of equity in your home exceeds your state's homestead exemption, you may still be able to prevent the creditors from forcing its sale. In a Chapter 13 filing (or where applicable, a Chapter 12 filing), you might be able to in effect "buy back" the excess amount of equity by paying that amount to your debtors over a period of time.

Using the example in which the house is worth $80,000, you still owe $51,500 to the bank holding your mortgage, and your state exempts $10,000 of home ownership, the remaining $18,500 can be paid in small monthly payments to your creditors. With this kind of plan, you can keep the house, and your creditors can still receive money to repay your debts. Of course much depends on your ability to prove that you can reasonably be expected to maintain both your monthly mortgage payment and the monthly payment of the excess equity, and still survive financially. Without such proof, the court will more than likely allow the sale of your home to satisfy your creditors' claims.

If You Had a Previous Bankruptcy

If you had debts discharged in a Chapter 7 bankruptcy, you will not be able to file again within six years from the date of the original filing. The date of your actual discharge does not affect this waiting period. If your Chapter 7 filing was dismissed because you requested a dismissal after a creditor successfully sought to vacate the automatic stay of creditors' actions that results from the filing, or you violated a court order, then you must wait 180 days before filing again.

In addition, any debts found nondischargeable in the previous filing cannot be included in the new filing.

If You Are Judgment Proof

The designation "judgment proof" applies to people in extremely bad financial condition with little hope of improving their lot for years to come. Being judgment proof means you own no property which can be seized for payment of debts,

Finding Alternatives To Bankruptcy

have little or no income that can be attached, and have limited prospects of improving this condition for at least several years.

If your situation fits this description, then filing bankruptcy will probably accomplish little for you since your creditors are going to have to write off your debts anyway. With this type of background it's unlikely you will get any new credit for a long time, so why bother going through the expense and trouble of filing bankruptcy?

Other Reasons Not to File Bankruptcy

If you believe you can repay your debts over three to five years and maintain a reasonable life-style, bankruptcy may not be best for you. The decision to file bankruptcy may be difficult for many people who feel a deep sense of obligation to pay their debts. They often overestimate their ability to meet even reduced monthly payments. If you believe you can repay the outstanding debts, provided your creditors agree to accept reduced payments, be sure to seek a professional opinion before agreeing to anything. Failure to do this may result in your agreeing to payment burdens that are realistically beyond your ability to carry.

If someone has co-signed a loan for you, you'll want to consider what your bankruptcy filing will do to them. Unless, as will be explained in Chapter 9, you file a Chapter 13 case, the creditor of a co-signed loan can go after your friend or relative for full payment if you file "straight" bankruptcy, so you may want to attempt to negotiate that loan separately before you file a Chapter 7 bankruptcy.

If you committed fraud in obtaining any credit, you face the possibility of those debts being excluded from your bankruptcy discharge. Examples of fraud are lying about your income or your indebtedness when applying for the credit or answering falsely any questions on a credit or loan application.

If you fall into any of these categories then you should consider a realistic alternative to bankruptcy.

WHEN AND HOW TO SETTLE OUT OF COURT

If your financial problems arise from one or two large debts, such as substantial child support obligations, an unliquidated claim for personal injury or breach of contract, or large medical bills, you may require legal assistance in resolving the cause of the debts before filing bankruptcy. Often one or two claimants with large debts are willing to settle for less or work out a realistic payment plan.

In many instances an out-of-court settlement based on a payment schedule that will not cripple your ability to lead an otherwise normal life is a much more satisfactory alternative. The principal caveat here is that a dissenting creditor is not bound by the agreements of other creditors. A single hostile creditor may scuttle the plan entirely.

Negotiating with multiple creditors, or creditors who are geographically widely dispersed, may prove so difficult as to make the entire process unworkable. A major danger, especially when negotiating with numerous creditors, is that one of them may take adverse action, such as seeking a judgment against you, while an agreement is being negotiated.

Historically, repayment agreements work best when the following factors are present:

- There are only a few creditors.
- Most creditors are unsecured.
- They are all in the same geographic area.
- The debtor has sufficient income or assets with which to make realistic payments.

Finding Alternatives To Bankruptcy

- The debtor does not need the emergency relief of an automatic stay of creditors' actions that comes with filing bankruptcy.

If these are major factors in your situation, you should consider the advantages of negotiating a settlement instead of filing bankruptcy.

How to Negotiate with Your Creditors

The best way to notify your creditors of your willingness to negotiate an out-of-court settlement is by telephone. If creditors are so numerous that telephoning them is impractical, negotiating and reaching agreements with them is probably also impractical.

It is advisable to negotiate a settlement quickly because it is usually necessary for you to disclose your nonexempt assets to your creditors. Delays may give a potential hostile or aggressive creditor the opportunity to make a claim against the exposed assets.

It is not necessary to treat all creditors alike. Even creditors with identical claims can be treated differently. Some creditors may be willing to accept substantially less than 100 percent of the amount owing them in return for early payment, while others will insist on the full amount even if it takes years of small payments.

A major pitfall in widely varied agreements could be the disclosure to all creditors of the terms on which each has agreed. Wide discrepancies in creditor treatment may cause negotiating difficulties. An experienced debtor/creditor negotiator will compute the debtor's liquidation value under a Chapter 7 bankruptcy and, if the numbers are appropriate, prorate the amount among the creditors so each unsecured creditor will know how little it will receive if an agreement isn't reached and the debtor is forced into bankruptcy. This is one of the many devices an experienced negotiator will use when dealing with creditors.

An agreement with creditors can be written so you make payments to each creditor, or you can make payments to someone who distributes the money to the creditors—commonly called a disbursing agent. The system selected depends on the number of creditors and the preferences of all parties. If a disbursing agent is chosen by the majority of creditors, it is best to use a major creditor or bank.

Use an Assignment for Benefit of Creditors

This is a method of repaying debts which usually involves transferring a debtor's assets to a third party known as an "assignee" who collects and sells the assets and distributes the proceeds among the creditors. It is most commonly used for debts incurred in connection with a business.

One advantage of this method is that it permits the prompt sale and distribution of assets. Another is that the debtor can control the designation of the assignee. Finally, there is generally less administrative effort than in a bankruptcy case. The main task of the assignee consists of the liquidation of assets, review of the claims, and the final distribution of money. Frequently no examination of witnesses is necessary, and there are no significant court proceedings which could prove costly in time and expenses. You should discuss this method of handling debts with an experienced attorney to see if it is appropriate for your circumstances.

WHERE TO FIND HELP

Widespread consumer credit is a phenomenon of the post–World War II era. By the mid-1960s buying on credit became a way of life for most Americans. Consumer credit was a driving force behind the growth and expansion of the Ameri-

Finding Alternatives To Bankruptcy

can economy. Credit was so easy to get that many banks sent unsolicited credit cards to consumers until that practice was outlawed.

It wasn't difficult to predict that along with the unprecedented growth of easy credit there would be a corresponding increase in the number of consumers who for one reason or another fell behind in their payments. Not far behind were the sharks, eager to pick at the wounded flesh of consumers in trouble. They went by high-sounding and helpful titles, such as "debt pro-raters," "debt adjusters," "debt consolidators," and "debt poolers."

Although there may have been some honest individuals among this pack, most were opportunists whose sole aim was to get as much money out of the already hurting debtor as possible by promising to resolve the individual's credit problems and persuade creditors to be more reasonable.

The way these people usually worked was to convince the already vulnerable debtor to sign a contract with the debt adjuster agreeing to make specific weekly payments. This money would presumably be distributed to the consumer's creditors under a plan to be agreed on by the debt adjuster and the creditors, less a fee the debt adjuster retained for the service.

The problem with most of these services was that creditors rarely agreed to the terms offered by the debt adjusters. In fact, a creditor contacted by a debt adjuster usually took the contact as evidence the consumer was in trouble and promptly moved to protect its interest through a wage attachment. Creditors willing to negotiate a repayment schedule often found themselves involved in prolonged haggling with the debt adjuster who was collecting money from the consumer, but delaying payments to the creditor.

As these debt service companies blossomed around the country, abuses grew worse. Some were found to have never paid any money to their customers' creditors before they suddenly closed their doors and left town with the money. The majority of consumers who used these debt adjustment services found their situation even worse than before.

By the late 1960s most states passed laws outlawing commercial debt adjustment companies. Meanwhile consumer debt continued to expand, and with it the number of people who fell behind in their payments grew, as did the number of people who ultimately sought the protection of the bankruptcy courts. Alarmed by the trend, the consumer credit industry took action in an attempt to stem the tide. Its response was to provide a legitimate service similar to that which the now-outlawed commercial debt adjusters claimed they provided to consumers.

The Truth About Consumer Counseling Services

Reacting to the burgeoning number of people who failed to pay their debts, the major creditors united to organize a "service" to help them collect their money. Under the control of the National Foundation for Consumer Credit (an association founded and funded by creditors), the network of affiliated Consumer Credit Counseling Services was created. Local offices can be found throughout the country. They are usually listed under the heading "Credit & Debt Counseling Services" in your local Yellow Pages.

Although these services operate on a not-for-profit basis, their employees are paid salaries and would appear to have a vested interest in enlisting as many people as possible for their debt management plans. While a few charge no fee for their services, most charge a nominal fee of between $10 and $20 per month.

A debtor seeking help from one of these services must first call for an appointment and then bring copies of pay

Finding Alternatives To Bankruptcy

stubs, outstanding bills, account numbers, and copies of letters from creditors to an initial meeting. A counselor reviews the paperwork, asks a series of questions, and then attempts to work out a program that requires the consumer to pay a predetermined amount, weekly or monthly, to the service. That payment, less a modest fee, is then distributed among the consumer's creditors.

The big "if" in the successful administration of these plans is to convince all creditors to agree. Obviously, a consumer credit counseling service funded and driven by creditors seeking to collect their money will have a better chance of getting creditors to agree to a repayment schedule than will an individual consumer or a commercial service. However, it requires only one hostile creditor to keep the plan from working. Since the counseling service alerts all creditors to the consumer's predicament, that lone hostile creditor could move quickly in obtaining a judgment against the consumer. The counseling service has no legal standing and cannot stop such an action.

The question inevitably arises about whose interests are best served by these consumer credit counseling services. Since they are for the most part funded by the credit industry, is it the creditor's or the debtor's interests they serve?

Experience shows that counseling services rarely, if ever, refer a consumer to an attorney or counselor specializing in personal bankruptcy or even discuss bankruptcy as a viable alternative. Their goal is to collect the consumer's debt in full. Bankruptcy would deny most or all the creditors a substantial amount or all of the money owed them.

A consumer who uses one of these counseling services should be aware that there may be a hidden agenda at work in a service that depends on the credit industry for its funding. Sometimes it is unwise, in the long term, to struggle for years to repay debt. The struggle may become so overwhelming that all other aspects of an individual's family life may suffer. Bankruptcy may be the correct path for a particular consumer; however, it is unlikely a credit counseling service will admit that.

Using a Bankruptcy Attorney

One of the authors of this book is an attorney specializing in bankruptcy matters. That is our disclosure statement. He did not participate in, and lend his expertise to, the writing of this book to solicit business for himself or his colleagues. He participated because he wanted people to understand that personal bankruptcy is not the end of an individual's life, but a realistic alternative which many people consider only when they have done so much damage to themselves and their self-esteem that it takes years for them to recover. The financial and credit consequences of bankruptcy may be small in comparison to the self-inflicted psychological wounds of many people struggling with debt so great that it cannot be repaid.

Credit difficulties and personal bankruptcy are far too important to trust to amateurs or emotionally involved friends or relatives. Professional help from someone who will represent your interests and do everything legally possible to protect you is essential. A competent bankruptcy attorney will explore every possibility to help a client avoid bankruptcy, but also knows when these efforts have been exhausted and when it is time to seek bankruptcy protection.

Chapter 12 will offer advice on selecting the right attorney. It would be redundant to restate that advice here, but it is extremely important that a debtor facing action from creditors find a professional who is knowledgeable of the applicable laws to provide protection from those actions. Any action taken against you by a creditor must be done through

Finding Alternatives To Bankruptcy

the courts and will require a legal defense, even if you never appear in court. It will cost more money than a counseling service, but this can definitely be a case of getting what you pay for.

A Do-It-Yourself Bankruptcy

The old adage that the person who defends himself has a fool for a client has never been more appropriate than in a bankruptcy case. Although several books have been published with instructions for filing bankruptcy forms, do-it-yourself is best left to fixing up your home or repairing your car. Too often people who take this approach in filing bankruptcy ultimately turn to a specialist after serious damage has been done.

While it is true that any literate person can fill out standardized forms, the value of expert legal opinion can mean the difference between success or failure when dealing with creditors or the court. Attorneys who specialize in other areas of the law turn to a bankruptcy attorney when they get into financial trouble because they know the value of expert representation. There are a small number of personal bankruptcies that can and are handled successfully on a do-it-yourself basis each year; however, these are usually cases without complications over property, support payments, hostile creditors, or creditors who challenge a debtor's filing or truthfulness. Complicated cases require someone expert in the law and knowledgeable in the practices of the local court.

By nature and training, attorneys are experienced negotiators who have the advantage of not being emotionally involved the way a debtor is. The attorney can be more objective than the client in most cases, especially when confronted with an attorney representing a creditor. In many respects, do-it-yourself bankruptcy is like do-it-yourself surgery and can produce similar results.

Four

HOW TO GET YOUR CREDITORS TO SETTLE FOR LESS

DETERMINING HOW MUCH YOU CAN PAY

If possible, it is definitely desirable to avoid bankruptcy by persuading your creditors to settle for less than the full amount owed them. While this may not always be possible, it is a viable alternative in many cases. A host of factors come into play when attempting to convince creditors to accept less than the amount owed. These include who your creditors are, how much money you owe them, their ability and willingness to close your account by taking less than the full amount due, and your ability to pay a reduced amount of your debt immediately.

Before presenting your creditors with a proposal to accept less money than you owe, or smaller payments over an extended period, you must determine how much you can pay. The creditor's first question after you suggest the possibility of a change in either the balance of your account or the size of your payments will probably be: "How much can you afford to pay?"

Simple Financial Formulas
The answer to this question requires some homework. To begin, jot down the amount of monthly or weekly disposable

income you have. This is the amount of take-home pay you receive from your job, plus any other income you receive on a regular basis, such as a part-time job. This must be cash you can definitely depend on, not income from an occasional weekend job or from selling items at a fair or flea market—unless you are a vendor at a flea market on a steady basis.

Make a list of your regular monthly or weekly expenses. This should include rent, utilities, mortgage payments, automobile payments, food, gas, telephone bill, insurance premiums, and dry cleaner bills, in other words, every ongoing expense that must be paid to continue to support you and your family. Be sure to leave a reasonable amount for entertainment and other items that contribute to worthwhile family life. Do not deny yourself or your family the small pleasures of life. If you do, you will regret having made a deal with your creditors from the start.

Now, subtract these necessary expenses from your disposable income, as shown in the following example:

EXAMPLE A

Your monthly disposable income		$3,200
Your necessary monthly expenses		2,700
Rent	$1,200	
Telephone	50	
Insurance	150	
Utilities	150	
Car payment	350	
Food	600	
Gas	100	
Other miscellaneous payments	100	
Amount available for creditor payments		$ 500

You *Can* Go Bankrupt *Without* Going Broke

If you subtract your necessary expenses from your disposable income and find there is no money left over, or worse, you are left with a negative figure, don't wait around brooding about your situation, contact a bankruptcy attorney immediately.

In Example A you have $500 left over each month to apply toward the payment of your loans and the outstanding balances on your credit card accounts. The next step is to total the amount you are currently required to pay each month to finance the outstanding debt and subtract that from what you have available.

EXAMPLE B

Amount available for creditor payments		$500
Total of outstanding monthly credit payments		850
VISA	$165	
Discover	125	
MasterCard	95	
Bank loan	200	
Local Department store	75	
Sears	150	
Finance company	40	
Amount you are short to make each monthly payment		$350

In Example B you have a shortfall of $350. This means that of the $850 you are presently obligated to pay your creditors each month, you are able to pay only $500, leaving $350 worth of payments that you cannot make.

Selecting the Right Creditors

Now you must decide which creditors you can approach personally and which you will contact by mail. Never attempt to bargain over the telephone. Prepare what you are going to ask the creditor to do for you. Do you want to reduce your monthly payments or reduce your balance? Keep in mind that any creditor confronted with a debtor having difficulty paying a debt will try to get as much money from the debtor as possible.

Individuals who find themselves in situations similar to those in Examples A and B generally do not have enough money in savings to offer a lump-sum payment to a creditor, but if for some reason you do, you can approach one or more creditors and suggest that if they are willing to accept less than the outstanding balance on your account, say, half, you are prepared to pay that amount in full, immediately. When a creditor accepts your offer, be sure you get a commitment in writing stating that the creditor will not report this transaction as negative information to any credit reporting agency. The creditor must also notify the credit agency that the account was paid and is now closed.

Actually, no law requires a lender or creditor to report negative information to a credit reporting agency. This is usually done voluntarily by the creditors for mutual protection. It is up to you to take full advantage of a creditor's willingness to cooperate with you and not report anything that will damage your credit standing. In fact, once a creditor has accepted any type of arrangement, you must ask that any negative information previously supplied a credit reporting agency be removed from your file. It may have already been reported that you missed several payments, or have been making late payments, so you will want that information deleted. Always make this your final request, after the lender or creditor has agreed to everything else. It is a minor request, and once your creditor has agreed to accept your money, he or she will not want to risk the arrangement over a point that is not too important to the company.

CONTACTING YOUR CREDITORS

It is generally advisable to establish and maintain an open line of communication with your creditors, especially if you intend to pay the money owed or anticipate negotiating with them soon. This may not always be possible, but you should do it whenever you can. Of course, if you decide to move to another state to protect your assets because you intend to file for bankruptcy, disregard open lines of communication.

Before you contact any creditor, be sure you have formulated your offer precisely. If you plan to offer a lump-sum payment for a reduced balance, be sure you have the money available immediately, not two weeks in the future. You will not know what kind of pressure and stress your creditor may be under, and you could be shocked by a quick agreement to your offer, providing you can make that lump-sum payment promptly. If you cannot make the payment you suggested right away, you may forfeit any agreement you made, so be prepared to deliver on your offer. If you visit the creditor in person, have your checkbook with you. Depending on how urgently your money is needed, your creditor may be willing to forgo a potentially greater future return and settle for a more immediate gain.

Once you have determined how much you can afford to pay your creditors, and you have formulated a plan, either a lump-sum payment in return for a reduced balance or reduced monthly payments, and you are fully prepared to meet the commitment you are suggesting, you are ready to confront your creditors.

Two avenues are open to you. The best is a face-to-face meeting with the creditor or an officer or other decision maker if the creditor is a company or bank. When this is not possible, as when a credit card issuer is located halfway across the country, it will be necessary to write. Remember, do not telephone a creditor. Odds are heavily against reaching a decision maker on the phone. You are far more likely to waste time and money in a fruitless explanation of your situation to a subordinate with no authority to do anything but cause you more problems. It is better to write. Even if your letter reaches a nondecision maker, since it is a written document that cannot simply be ignored, it will eventually be passed on to someone who has the authority to deal with you. A follow-up telephone call to check on the status of your letter is a good idea.

Meeting Your Creditor Face to Face

The first step in negotiating any change in your current payment schedule, interest rate, or balance due on an account is to size up the creditor. When doing this, remember that creditors are people, not brick buildings or marble facades with huge columns. If possible, sit face to face with someone at the company or institution to which you owe money. This tactic alters the existing relationship from one of an anonymous employee dealing with an anonymous debtor who is little more than an account number, to a person-to-person relationship.

When you meet with a creditor on a person-to-person basis you must learn to take advantage of the pressures that person may be under. Creditors do not want to lose money. Companies and lending institutions frown on employees who cause them to lose it. The individual you meet with has an obligation, as an employee who desires to stay in his or her manager's good graces, to prevent that from happening.

Debtors who stop making their payments cause two things to happen to a creditor or lending institution. The first is a reduction of cash flow. This may not sound drastic, until you consider that many creditors deal with thousands of debtors. At any given time a percentage of those debtors have difficulty meeting their obligations. The company's goal is to reduce that percentage as much as possible. On average more than $60 million in personal debts in this country is overdue at any time. Because of this it is easy to understand why creditors worry about late or missed payments.

A second situation resulting from a debtor's failure to make payments is that the creditor runs the risk of losing money. Even if the debtor has property that can be repossessed or foreclosed on, the chances are high that the creditor will lose money when all the expenses, including legal fees and resale costs, are calculated. The odds are against the creditor recovering anything close to the amount of money it would have realized had the debtor continued making payments. It is generally in the creditor's best interest to make whatever reasonable arrangements it can to facilitate repayment of the amount owed, plus the interest charges.

An important point to remember when negotiating with a creditor or lending institution is that you want to remain in control of the situation. You are approaching the creditor with an arrangement that, if you have prepared your proposal properly, will create a win-win situation. You do not want a creditor to see your suggestion as creating a situation in which you are the winner and it is the loser. You should convey the attitude that you want to do whatever you can to meet your obligations, but you are now in debt over your head and are willing to pay what you can, if the creditor is willing to cooperate with you.

Do not be deterred by a creditor who appears at first to refuse to make any concessions about your obligation. Keep in mind that the person you are speaking with probably hears a dozen sad stories every day from people who are unable to make their payments. Most of those debtors come hat in hand with the attitude that they are in trouble financially and the creditor should understand this and give them sympathy. Creditors are not social service agencies or charities; they do not give sympathy. They expect to be paid back, with interest.

Your attitude clearly should be that you cannot meet your present obligation and that it is in the best interest of the creditor to work out an arrangement that will benefit you both. Explain that you have reviewed your current financial condition and worked out a plan that you hope the creditor will agree to which will enable you to meet at least a portion of your obligation. Then explain your suggestion. If you are offering to make a lump-sum payment in return for a reduction in the amount you owe so that your payment pays the account off, be sure the creditor understands you can make that payment today. The creditor may decide that a bird in the hand is worth much more than two in the bush, especially if there is a good chance the two in the bush may fly away. If you convince the creditor that your financial condition is such that there is a possibility you may have to file bankruptcy, and the creditor could receive less than you are offering, or possibly nothing, your offer will appear all the more attractive.

Even if bankruptcy is not in the offing, a creditor who cannot collect will usually turn such an account over to a collection agency. The collection agency receives a percentage of what it collects from debtors, frequently as much as 40 percent. That means if the collection agency is able to collect the full amount of your debt, the best the creditor can expect if 60 cents on the dollar. The situation becomes worse if the collection agency is unable to retrieve the full amount of your debt. Since collection agencies are paid only after their services get results, they are highly motivated to settle for less than the full amount owed. Suppose the collection agency is able to convince you to pay three quarters of your debt in return for closing the account. The creditor must now settle for substantially less than you may have offered in your original proposal. It could well be in the creditor's best interest to accept half of what you owe right now and not go through the trouble of dealing with a collection agency.

Perhaps a more practical reason a creditor is willing to deal with you instead of a collection agency is that debt collectors are successful in collecting only about 20 percent of the debt assigned to them by creditors. This means a creditor will usually be forced to write off about 80 percent of the debts it turns over to a collection agency for action.

An alternative to making a proposal to your creditor is to solicit the creditor's advice and assistance in arriving at a solution to what you see as a *temporary* problem. Do not fail to emphasize that your financial difficulties are only temporary. This approach usually works well with local creditors such as town banks and local mortgage lenders. After discussing fully what has brought you to your current situation, ask the person with whom you are meeting for advice on options which might be available to see you through this temporarily difficult time. If possible it is always helpful to discuss your situation with the individual who originally approved your loan. That person has a vested personal interest in preventing your loan from falling into default.

Local bankers and other creditors in the community appreciate a debtor who treats them respectfully and honestly. Asking their advice appeals to their egos and will go a long way toward identifying some options of which you might not be aware. The banker or creditor may choose to share them with you because of the straightforward professional manner in which you handle the situation without attempting to elicit sympathy for your financial woes.

Remember, no one likes dealing with a loser. If you try to whine your way into a situation where you hope a creditor will pity you and offer help, you are wasting time and jeopardizing an opportunity to solve your problem. If you demonstrate, through your attitude and the questions you ask, that you have intelligently thought out the situation and honestly seek a solution that is fair to all parties, your chances of winning the creditor over will be much greater.

Once the creditor acknowledges that it might be possible to make a different arrangement, go to the lowest number you feel is reasonable and stick to it. Suppose you are willing and able to write a check today for three quarters of what you owe; begin by offering the creditor one-half of the balance on your account if the creditor will accept that as payment in full. The creditor indicates that one-half is not enough, but a deal might be possible if you split the difference between what you owe and what you offered to pay. It is suggested by the creditor that if you pay three quarters of your account, it will be considered paid in full. The creditor has just acknowledged that he or she can go lower if you demonstrate that this is the only way to clear the account. Treat the three quarters amount as the creditor's first offer, and explain you just cannot raise the additional amount right now, but you might be able to squeeze a few more dollars out if the creditor is willing to split the difference between the suggested three quarters and the one-half you can pay.

Example

The total debt you owe this creditor is	$1,000
The amount you claim you are able to pay	$500
The amount the creditor wants you to pay by splitting the difference	$750
The amount you offer to pay by splitting the difference between your offer and the creditor's offer	$625

You *Can* Go Bankrupt *Without* Going Broke

Since few of us are expert at conducting important negotiations, we recommend strongly that you visit the nearest library and read at least one or two of the more popular books on negotiating. You will be amazed at just how far you can get with a creditor if you sharpen your negotiating skills. The creditor probably spends a good portion of each day negotiating with people who want to pay less than they owe, so you are going up against someone who has expertise in negotiating skills. Unless you develop your own skills, you will be at a distinct disadvantage.

Regardless of the lack of success of your first meeting with a creditor, do not cease negotiating. Always be willing to meet again. You can never tell what might move a seemingly immovable creditor. Perhaps the day after your meeting a few notices of personal bankruptcy filings by debtors will arrive and the creditor will decide you might follow suit. The creditor may suddenly feel it is better to agree to an offer that realizes some cash rather than take a chance you will become the proverbial stone from which he will get no blood.

It may be possible to effect a change of heart in a creditor who is unwilling to negotiate by following your initial unsuccessful meeting with a brief letter thanking the creditor for taking the time to meet with you. Express your disappointment at not arriving at a workable solution to the problem, and restate the offer you made. Given some time, and perhaps a change in the creditor's circumstances, you might be surprised to receive a telephone call from the previously uncooperative creditor asking you to come in to discuss your offer.

Under no conditions agree to a repayment plan that exceeds the amount of money you have available. This will only mean you will eventually find once again that you cannot meet your obligations. Creditors who have previously granted a change in your payment schedule are unlikely to accommodate you a second time. It is far better to agree to a realistic plan the first time.

You can always sweeten your offer with the promise of increasing your payments when your financial situation improves. Of course, should your financial picture improve, it is incumbent on you to live up to your promise and increase the amount of your payments. When you do, be sure to write to the person to whom you made this pledge, advising him or her of the increase. This might go a long way if you ever apply for another loan or credit with that individual in the future.

Five

WHEN BANKRUPTCY IS THE ONLY WAY OUT

CLASSIFYING YOUR DEBTS

When Pat Dillon left his secure middle management position with a large corporation to open a small retail store, he thought he had saved enough money to set up the business and cover his expenses for a reasonable period of time. Pat's money ran out as the preparations for opening the business neared completion. Unable to raise additional cash from friends and relatives, Pat turned to the single other source of ready cash available to him, his credit cards. Because of his excellent credit rating, Pat had accumulated more than a half dozen VISA and MasterCards. He began withdrawing small sums from the cash advance privileges provided by the accounts. Pat expected to repay the advances from the salary he planned to draw from the business.

That was the beginning of a two-year financial nightmare that ultimately culminated in bankruptcy for Pat. Although the business was moderately successful during its two years, Pat was never able to draw enough money to support

When Bankruptcy is the Only Way Out

himself and repay the cash advances. Finally, in 1986 Pat joined over 400,000 Americans who filed for bankruptcy protection.

Before resorting to bankruptcy Pat tried but failed to persuade his creditors to understand his plight and participate in a workable repayment plan that would allow his business to survive. He was forced to close the business and went to work for a salary considerably lower than he had previously earned, even further limiting his ability to repay the cash advances.

Pat had even less success with the banks which had issued his credit cards. He received little or no response and was frequently unable to contact anyone with whom he could negotiate a repayment plan. Letters went unanswered and telephone calls seldom got beyond clerks who told him he must pay his bill on time or else.

If Pat had thought to consult a credit counseling service at this time, he might not have filed for bankruptcy. A representative at a competent counseling service would know whom to contact at each bank and might have been able to arrange a suitable repayment plan.

Another alternative for Pat would have been to contact an attorney specializing in credit problems. An attorney with the authority to negotiate could have taken the steps necessary to get the attention of bank officials, or he might have recommended that Pat file for bankruptcy. The attorney's recommendation would depend on an assessment of Pat's chances to recover from his debts and make a fresh start.

Pat's decision to file for bankruptcy was actually his best choice. All his debts were quickly discharged in bankruptcy. Since he owned no nonexempt assets, his creditors received no money in payment for the outstanding balances of his accounts. Pat was able to begin working toward his "fresh start" the day following the receipt of his bankruptcy discharge.

You *Can* Go Bankrupt *Without* Going Broke

Had Pat attempted to repay the money he owed, he would have been burdened with heavy monthly payments for years. While it is true that credit reports would show he had filed bankruptcy, which could prevent him from obtaining new credit for up to ten years, it is questionable that his credit files, already damaged by his failure to make timely payments on his accounts, could have been cleaned up so he could get fresh credit during the time he was making payments on the old accounts.

Many times bankruptcy is not only the best way out of a serious credit problem, but the only way out. While we don't encourage anyone to take the step of filing for bankruptcy protection lightly, we do encourage you to seek the advice of an attorney when you recognize that your financial obligations have become an intolerable burden.

Before the time of Christ, the Roman Law of the Twelve Tables decreed that a man who was indebted to several creditors, and unable to repay his debt, faced the prospect of having his body cut up into several pieces and distributed among his creditors. This may have seemed at times like a kind of macabre relief for some people overwhelmed by the enormity of their debt, but it obviously served no one. The debtor died, and the creditors found themselves with useless decaying body parts instead of the money owed them by the unfortunate debtor.

If there was a single creditor, the debtor could be either put to death or made a slave until the debt was repaid through his labors. Although not entirely satisfying, the latter approach was greatly preferred by most debtors.

We can all be grateful that society now takes a kinder view of people who are unable to repay their debts. By virtue of our bankruptcy laws, society's attitude toward debtors is far more sympathetic. This sympathy is undoubtedly born from a feeling of affinity by so many people in this credit-

When Bankruptcy is the Only Way Out

driven system who live uncomfortably close to the brink of bankruptcy themselves.

The framers of the Constitution considered the issue of bankruptcy sufficiently important to reserve it to the federal government instead of leaving it for the states to control. The U.S. Congress was given the power to make "uniform laws" on bankruptcy which supersede any insolvency laws the individual states may establish. As a result, all petitions for bankruptcy, individual or corporate, are filed in a federal court, the bankruptcy court.

Dischargeable Debts

One important power left to the states in bankruptcy cases is the determination of what property an individual in such a case can claim as exempt and which cannot be taken to satisfy creditors. These laws vary widely, as you will see from reviewing the information in Chapters 10 and 11.

The different ways in which states protect the assets of those filing for bankruptcy have created a patchwork of laws, some more lenient than others. One result is that some states, notably Florida and Texas, have become magnets for individuals planning to file bankruptcy. *The Wall Street Journal* recently referred to Florida as a haven for debtors. No statistics are available on exactly how many people have moved to Florida because of its debtor protection rules, but a whopping increase in Florida bankruptcies strongly indicates that a great many people have chosen to establish residency in the "Sunshine State" in anticipation of claiming bankruptcy.

The nationwide increase in bankruptcy filings rose by a little more than 200 percent from 1980 to 1989. During the same period bankruptcy filings in Florida skyrocketed by over 650 percent. The practice of establishing residency in Florida before filing for bankruptcy received widespread notoriety through reports of several wealthy individuals who suddenly became Floridians. These included former baseball commissioner Bowie Kuhn who sold his New Jersey home for $1 million and moved to Ponte Vedra Beach, Florida, just before his New York law firm went belly up. Under New York law, partners like Kuhn could be held personally responsible for the debts of their partnership.

Another famous example of fleeing to Florida for protection was that of Marvin Warner of the failed Ohio-based Home State Savings Bank, who quickly sold his Ohio horse farm and purchased a 160-acre horse farm near Ocala, Florida, for $2.2 million. Taking full advantage of Florida laws, Warner was able to protect some $6 million in assets from his creditors when his bank collapsed.

In Ohio Mr. Warner could have claimed a homestead exemption of only $10,000. Florida's debtor protection laws permit a person filing bankruptcy to shield a home from creditors provided it is the principal residence, no matter what its value. The only limitation is the size of the property. If the home is located within a city, it can occupy no more than ½ acre. Homesteads outside city limits can be as large as Mr. Warner's 160-acre horse farm.

Florida residents have other protection besides their homes. Assets beyond the reach of creditors include the head of household's salary, annuities, retirement and profit-sharing funds, and individual retirement accounts (IRAs). According to reliable reports, Mr. Warner was able to protect over $3 million in cash by investing it in annuities, a benefit he would not have enjoyed in his previous state of residence, Ohio.

Although not as forgiving as Florida, most states provide some degree of protection to debtors. Chapters 10 and 11 give you all the information needed to determine what portion of your assets are protected by the laws of your state. Chapter 13 gives sound advice on how to protect your assets when you file bankruptcy.

When Bankruptcy is the Only Way Out

If bankruptcy is a viable option for you, the first step is to get professional legal advice. An attorney who specializes in bankruptcy can review your current situation thoroughly, explain what options are available to you, and recommend a course of action. A certain amount of what is known as "prepetition planning" is acceptable. Such planning may save you much more than the attorney's fee, both financially and psychologically.

Nondischargeable Debts

When considering bankruptcy as an option, the advantages and disadvantages must be clearly understood. Before reviewing these however, let's first take a look at some debts that will not be discharged by filing bankruptcy. They are called nondischargeable debts or debts you will still owe even after you receive a bankruptcy discharge. These nondischargeable debts are set by federal law and apply in all states. A second category of debts may be nondischargeable, depending, in some cases, on the actions of your creditors.

Among the nondischargeable debts are

1. most federal, state, and local taxes
2. recent student loans
3. child and spousal support
4. debts not discharged in a previous bankruptcy because of misfeasance or fraud
5. government fines and penalties
6. court judgments arising from driving while under the influence of drugs or alcohol

We can add to this any debts you did not list on your bankruptcy schedules. A bankruptcy filing cannot discharge a debt that was not listed.

When the bankruptcy court issues an order granting

You *Can* Go Bankrupt *Without* Going Broke

your bankruptcy discharge, it states that you are released from "all dischargeable debts." This means if any of your debts fall into one of the six categories listed, they will not be discharged and the creditor is free to take legal action against you.

Debts That May Be Nondischargeable

There are three other categories of debt that may also be considered nondischargeable, depending on the actions of your creditors. These are

1. fraudulently incurred debts
2. debts resulting from your having willfully or maliciously caused damage to another's person or property
3. debts resulting from fraud while acting in a fiduciary capacity, larceny, or embezzlement

However, unless a creditor files a complaint with the bankruptcy court regarding their dischargeability, these types of debts may automatically be included as "dischargeable debts."

> When Thomas Graves began to fall behind in his loan and credit card payments shortly after losing his job, he quickly realized his debts were far greater than he was going to be able to repay. His job as a handyman at a nearby apartment complex didn't pay much, but that did not prevent him from acquiring numerous credit cards, usually by overstating his income. When Thomas decided that he would have to file bankruptcy to get his creditors off his back, he also decided to get all he could from the credit card issuers that had not yet canceled his accounts. He went on a spending spree fully expecting he would never have to pay for the purchases he charged on these credit card accounts.

When Bankruptcy is the Only Way Out

Like many other people, Thomas had the common misconception that all his debts would be discharged by filing bankruptcy. He didn't realize that some of his debts could fall into the category of nondischargeable debts, should they be challenged by his creditors. Because Thomas gave false income information to obtain three credit cards, all the debts outstanding on those three accounts could have been found nondischargeable since they fell within the first category—"fraudulently incurred debts." Thomas was lucky that none of the three banks that had issued the cards challenged his bankruptcy filing.

Thomas was less fortunate with his second action, charging purchases on his credit cards when he knew he was not going to pay for them. One card he used was a charge account at a local retail shop. When the owner of the store, who knew Thomas personally, learned of the bankruptcy filing, he immediately filed a complaint with the court specifying his objection. On examining the facts as presented by the retailer, the bankruptcy judge ruled the debt nondischargeable because it had been fraudulently incurred. Thus, the store owner was free to take whatever legal remedies were available to recover the money Thomas owed.

Many people make the mistake of increasing their debts when they never intend to repay them. This is a dangerous action which restricts the ability of these people, if discovered, to make a fresh start after their bankruptcy. Filing bankruptcy and admitting you cannot repay your debts is a difficulty you don't want to exacerbate by adding fraud to the equation. If you have deliberately run up charge accounts while planning bankruptcy, as Thomas did, be certain to confide that to the attorney. An experienced bankruptcy attorney will know the proper legal actions to take to provide you with as much protection as possible.

You *Can* Go Bankrupt *Without* Going Broke

THE ADVANTAGES OF PERSONAL BANKRUPTCY

The principal goal of a bankruptcy filing is to give the debtor relief from debts. The result of a successful bankruptcy filing is that the debtor is released from the requirement of paying debts. In the legal term, the debts are "discharged." The discharge of your debts is the final result of bankruptcy. But certain advantages are obtained immediately on filing a bankruptcy petition. These include

- stopping creditor harassment
- protecting your property
- centralizing and formalizing dealings with creditors
- halting all legal actions by creditors

We will take a closer look at each of these so you fully understand the advantages to filing bankruptcy.

Stop Creditors from Harassing You

A debtor being harassed by creditors will generally find filing a bankruptcy petition a swift and effective way to end that harassment. The bankruptcy petition prevents creditors from attaching part of your salary each pay day. Although in most states the law limits the percentage of a salary that can be taken to satisfy a judgment, filing for bankruptcy will spare the embarrassment of having your employer learn your creditors are pressing you.

Bankruptcy will also help reduce the anxiety with which most overburdened debtors live. The marital stress and discord created by unpaid bills or too many bills can be eased through a bankruptcy filing that usually reduces family tension and helps hold the family together.

Protect Your Property

Bankruptcy is often the only way a debtor can protect

When Bankruptcy is the Only Way Out

property that creditors might otherwise seize as payment for debts. Property used as collateral for a debt is treated differently. This is called a secured debt. We will discuss secured debts later in this chapter.

Although many states have laws protecting a debtor's property from an unsecured creditor, the protection is never as great as that afforded by a petition for bankruptcy. Bankruptcy frequently provides a debtor total protection against creditors seizing a home, automobile, or other property.

Control Your Dealings with Creditors

Instead of six creditors coming at you from six different directions, filing a bankruptcy petition forces them to work through the bankruptcy court. They will also be forced to abide by the rulings of the bankruptcy judge and to attend a meeting of all creditors having a claim against you.

It will be necessary for corporate creditors such as banks, loan companies, and department stores to incur the cost of legal fees to represent their interests as creditors, including having an attorney attend the meeting of creditors. Generally, at this point many creditors drop out of the process and write off the debt if the amount they expect to recover doesn't justify the costs involved.

Halt Legal Action by Creditors

It would not be unusual for those six creditors to be bringing action in six different courts. When creditors realize a debt is not going to be paid through normal means, they usually move quickly to obtain a judgment before other creditors do.

The first place most creditors go to is your salary. Because they know they are limited to a relatively small fraction of your salary (depending on the law in your state), creditors who have decided to take legal action to collect their money follow the axiom "the early bird gets the worm." The creditor who gets a judgment and places a garnishee against your salary first gets the money. Latecomers must wait until the first creditor has been paid.

A bankruptcy filing must list the name, address, account number, and amount owed to each creditor. Every creditor on that list is notified of the bankruptcy filing and of the requirement that all legal actions against you for collection of debts be suspended and that all future actions on the creditor's part be funneled through the bankruptcy court.

Many people do not want their employer to know of their financial problems and are fearful their wages may be attached by a creditor. Yet the same people will wait until their employer has received several garnishments against their salary before speaking to an attorney who specializes in resolving such matters. Too many debtors who should consider bankruptcy as a realistic alternative postpone the decision to seek help longer than they should. This causes unnecessary legal actions against them and undue psychological pressures.

Filing for bankruptcy brings the debtor an enormous relief, a relief that allows a "breathing space." The creditors are held off, and the debtor is given the opportunity to regroup and proceed with life.

The automatic stay obtained by the filing of a bankruptcy petition immediately stops most creditor actions, including lawsuits, repossessions, garnishments or attachments, utility shut-offs, foreclosures, and evictions. When you file a bankruptcy petition, you effectively halt all collection efforts by your creditors.

The purpose of halting all creditor activities is to provide a breathing spell, a chance to sort things out and assess your financial problems. Sometimes an attorney can use this time to convince previously uncooperative creditors to agree to work out a realistic solution to the debtor's problems. It is

When Bankruptcy is the Only Way Out

surprising how many creditors are willing to settle for a lot less than they are owed when a debtor files for bankruptcy and creditors face the possibility of getting nothing.

The automatic stay is so strong that violating it subjects the creditor to being held in contempt of court. Sometimes the stay may entitle the petitioner to retain a driver's license which is subject to revocation because of an unpaid judgment, although the license may once again face revocation after the judgment has been discharged in a bankruptcy case.

An individual facing a contempt citation arising from failure to pay court-ordered family support, either spousal support or child support payments, may find that although these are nondischargeable debts, the automatic stay may prevent the contempt order from resulting in arrest.

All these advantages are temporary, pending the outcome of the bankruptcy case. If your bankruptcy discharge is granted, you will be released from paying all the debts you listed when the petition was filed, provided

1. none of the debts is considered nondischargeable
2. a creditor did not successfully challenge the filing
3. you did not give the court false information

Although there are disadvantages to filing for bankruptcy, which we will discuss next, the individual who files for protection under the bankruptcy laws, just like a corporation that does the same, is no longer considered a pariah to be avoided at all costs.

Corporate and personal bankruptcy filings grew dramatically during the boom years of the 1980s, and there is every indication the trend will continue during the 1990s and beyond. During the past decade major corporations in almost every industry, from Braniff Airways to Seatrain to Toys "Я" Us, successfully sought bankruptcy court protection and survived. The number of individuals filing for protection will soon reach one million a year and include a vast number of ordinary working people who have gotten into debt over their heads, as well as the famous high rollers whose bankruptcies make the evening news, such as the sons of the late H. L. Hunt, once the richest man in the world, and John Connally, former governor of Texas, cabinet officer, and presidential candidate.

A comparison of corporate and individual bankruptcy is appropriate, because in the not-too-distant past both were viewed with distaste by society. Today a corporation operating under the rules of a Chapter 11 bankruptcy case can continue to do business in an otherwise normal manner, including receiving credit from suppliers and obtaining funds from the financial community. An individual who has turned to the bankruptcy court for protection also continues to live an otherwise normal life. The reality is that while credit may not be as easy to get as it once was, which might not be all that bad, it is still available, as we discuss in the final chapter of this book.

So many people have filed for bankruptcy during the last two decades that is is difficult to imagine anyone who does not know at least one person who has done so. This personal intimacy with bankruptcy, coupled with the fact most people purchase items they could not afford without incurring some debt, has mollified the attitudes of previous generations.

Unlike previous generations, we live in a consumer-oriented society propelled by credit. Without credit we could not afford most of the large, expensive, or luxury items we own. Without credit we would still be living as our grandparents did, buying something we want or need only when we have the cash. Before credit became an integral part of our existence, bankruptcy was a mark on a person's character and ability to conduct his or her life appropriately. Along with the acceptance of extended credit to purchase cars, furniture, jewelry, appliances, and almost everything else has come an acceptance of personal bankruptcy, when a person needs a fresh start. One bankruptcy attorney called personal bankruptcy the Federal Fresh Start Program.

While bankruptcy is no longer odious, there are disadvantages that must be examined by anyone who considers it as a way to deal with overwhelming debt.

THE DISADVANTAGES OF PERSONAL BANKRUPTCY

The familiar saying "there is no free lunch" means everything has a cost. Bankruptcy is no exception. Before filing for bankruptcy, a debtor should be aware of the costs involved. By this we don't mean simply attorney or filing fees; we mean what the bankruptcy will cost financially and psychologically, now and in the future. Asking a court to release you from financial obligations is obviously a decision that must carry a variety of consequences; and not all are happy ones. But they can be dealt with successfully. Let us look at some of the disadvantages of bankruptcy.

You May Lose Your Property
One possible consequence is the loss of any nonexempt property you may own. Studies have shown this is not a major problem for people filing Chapter 7 bankruptcy because few own nonexempt property. (For complete descriptions of the various forms of bankruptcy, see Chapters 6 through 9.) Those filing a Chapter 13 bankruptcy case are apt to find they will often be able to keep all their possessions.

The definition of which property qualifies as exempt or nonexempt varies widely across the country. Most states require that the individual state's definition of exempt property be used, while some allow the debtor to choose either the local definition or the federal definition of exemption. Appendix A clarifies which exemption definition may be used in each state and what the exemptions are.

How It Will Affect Your Mortgage

Owning your own home is the typical American dream. Home ownership carries with it a certain degree of respectability and social status. For most of us it also brings a sizable debt which must be repaid every month for years to come. The American preoccupation with home and land ownership can be traced to Thomas Jefferson who wrote that private ownership of land was the basic republican virtue and an important bulwark against tyranny.

Home mortgages and some other types of debts secured by a home or other real property are treated differently from other secured debts in the bankruptcy process. As eloquent testimony to the powerful political influence of banks and other mortgage lenders, the bankruptcy code specifically identifies home mortgages as requiring treatment different from other secured debts which may be subject to alteration in payment sizes and schedules.

Should you be faced with the decision of which debts to pay next month, and which to defer because your income no longer equals your monthly bills, your mortgage payment must be at, or at least near, the top of your list. Financial problems, and even bankruptcy, can cause severe psychological damage to any family, but the worst damage can result from being literally thrown out of your own home because you are unable to pay the mortgage. It is a humiliating and devastating experience. Of course, we hope that before you reach this stage, you have consulted a professional who may be able to stem your downward slide and help you repair and rebuild your financial status.

When Bankruptcy is the Only Way Out

An increasing number of personal bankruptcy attorneys are affiliated with a psychologist or similar counseling professional who specializes in helping people in financial difficulty, or who have filed bankruptcy, deal with the psychological and emotional aspects of the experience.

What Happens to Your Credit Standing

A major drawback to filing bankruptcy is that the discharge of your debts will be listed in your file with the companies that collect, maintain, and sell information about all of us. These companies are called "consumer reporting agencies." The information they sell to creditors, insurers, employers, and others is called a "consumer report." The term "agency" used to identify these companies that operate for a profit is a misnomer, since it implies that they have official standing. It would be more appropriate if they were called "consumer reporting companies" or other similarly less imposing titles.

By the time most people reach a point where they must seriously consider bankruptcy as a viable solution to their financial difficulties, they have already felt pressure from many, if not all, of their creditors. These creditors may have already routinely notified the consumer reporting agencies of the late or failed payments. This information is then readily available to almost any company willing to pay for it.

If the information placed in your file by these unhappy creditors is considered damaging enough by another prospective creditor, you may be denied credit. When an attorney or other professional reviews your situation, one important factor that is taken into consideration is your consumer report. If your credit standing is already badly damaged, and your creditors will not agree to retract the information they provided concerning your current problems, then the prospect of adding bankruptcy to your file will probably have little added effect on your credit standing.

You *Can* Go Bankrupt *Without* Going Broke

On the other hand, should your creditors agree to a workable repayment schedule, and pledge to remove all damaging information they placed in your credit file, that might be a more desirable alternative. Short of that, once your debts have been discharged, that fact will be recorded in your file and possibly sold to any future creditor, insurer, or potential or current employer.

Information about your bankruptcy will remain a part of your consumer credit file for a minimum of seven years and a maximum of ten years.

The Impact on Your Future Credit

There is no question that once a person files a bankruptcy case the individual's credit rating will be seriously damaged. Acquiring new credit will be more difficult, but not impossible. In Chapter 14 we discuss ways in which you can obtain new credit during your fresh start.

But the news is not all bad. Experience shows that while all potential creditors and lenders look askance at a credit report with late and failed payments, judgments, and salary attachments, some of them look more kindly on a bankruptcy. This is especially true if you can demonstrate to a prospective creditor that your bankruptcy was the result of a business failure, a medical catastrophe, or some other unexpected incident which was beyond your normal ability to control.

Many creditors make their decision to extend credit based primarily on an applicant's current income and stability. Some creditors will approve an applicant with a bankruptcy history if income, stability, an appraisal of the applicant's credit history other than the bankruptcy, and an understanding of the cause of the bankruptcy are carefully reviewed. Another factor that may help you find new credit is that once your debts have been discharged in a Chapter 7 bankruptcy case, you cannot file a bankruptcy case again for six years. This offers new creditors a degree of protection against the loss they might suffer if you were allowed to file bankruptcy sooner.

We do not wish to minimize the negative effect bankruptcy can have on your future ability to obtain credit; a credit report with no damaging information is far more preferable. Most creditors will gladly remove negative information from your file if they are assured they can recoup at least some of the money owed them. If you are able to do this, it is unquestionably the best alternative. Negotiating this type of arrangement with a creditor is best done by a third party, such as an attorney or credit counselor, who is less likely to be emotionally involved in your credit standing than you are and is capable of protecting you from a vindictive creditor.

About Your Personal Reputation

People are not going to follow you around pointing you out as a bankrupt person to strangers. You will not be required to wear a sign or be branded with a red "B" so everyone knows you failed to repay your debts. In fact, your friends, relatives, people you work with, or the company you work for need never know you filed bankruptcy, unless you tell them.

Despite this, many people who have had their debts discharged in bankruptcy brand themselves psychologically. For these individuals, this is the single most devastating aspect of bankruptcy. Before filing for bankruptcy you may have held the hope, no matter how unrealistic, that you would be able to find a way to pay your debts. That hope is abandoned when a bankruptcy case is filed. While it is true that bankruptcy is a form of admission that you don't think you will ever be able to meet your debts, it is not a reason to diminish your own self-worth.

You *Can* Go Bankrupt *Without* Going Broke

Bankruptcy is a by-product of a society that has, in effect, replaced hard currency with credit as the primary means of exchanging goods and services. A still small but increasing number of establishments do not want to be paid with cash. They prefer checks or credit cards. Part of the reason is that robbers want cash, not checks or MasterCard stubs. But there has to be more to it. An Allstate Insurance Company office located in an affluent neighborhood of Westchester County, New York, an area with little crime, has a sign in the window stating they do not accept insurance premium payments in cash, a sign of things to come.

It is ironic that many of the people appearing on television talk shows or in interviews with reporters about credit problems who claim to be shocked by the number of Americans turning to the bankruptcy courts for protection represent the same lending institutions that helped make us a credit-driven society. Until they were stopped by federal law, many of them used the mail to distribute tens of thousands of unsolicited credit cards to people who never wanted them. They have little reason to be shocked, since the growth in personal bankruptcies is, at least, partially traceable to their own previous loose credit policies.

Most bankruptcy cases do not seriously damage the debtor's reputation. The exception might be in a small town where the creditors whose debts are discharged are largely local merchants. They may harbor some temporary resentment as a result of the bankruptcy. Other than that, the remainder of your life is in your hands.

YOUR NEXT STEP

Everyone has the right to file bankruptcy. There is no minimum debt load, no debt-to-asset ratio, no requirement that your debts be greater than income, no requirement that

When Bankruptcy is the Only Way Out

you be penniless, and no requirement that you be prepared to turn all your worldly possessions over to your creditors.

The U.S. Supreme Court has said bankruptcy "relieves the honest debtor from the weight of the oppressive and often unfair indebtedness and permits him a fresh start." If you are an honest debtor facing oppressive debts, don't permit them to ruin your life, and possibly wreck your family. You should look at bankruptcy as a legal and accepted solution that offers you a way out and gives you the chance to make a fresh start.

Get Competent Help

Several times in this book we speak of your relationship with an attorney. We cannot emphasize this strongly enough because we firmly believe that bankruptcy is a step of such monumental importance that although it may be possible to file a do-it-yourself bankruptcy petition, it doesn't make sense to do so without professional help. Our goal here is not to solicit clients for bankruptcy attorneys, but to help you understand what bankruptcy can and cannot do for you.

A competent bankruptcy attorney will not simply push you into bankruptcy, but counsel and advise you of all the alternatives available to you. The attorney's role is more than that of a technician who fills out forms. A good bankruptcy attorney must be a counselor who helps the debtor deal not only with the financial aspects of bankruptcy, but the emotional and psychological aspects as well.

BANKRUPTCY, CHAPTER BY CHAPTER

The bankruptcy terms Chapter 7, Chapter 11, and Chapter 13 are almost household expressions, but most people do not understand the differences between these distinct provisions of the bankruptcy laws. Even less known, especially among those living in cities and suburban areas, is Chapter 12. In the following chapters we clarify these forms of bankruptcy and explain the procedures involved in each.

A person considering bankruptcy whose financial situation arises almost exclusively from consumer debt must be informed of the options available when filing under the various chapters. In fact, the bankruptcy petition is required to include a clear statement from the attorney affirming that the client has been informed of those options. This rule exists to protect clients from an unscrupulous or incompetent attorney who might rush into filing under an inappropriate chapter for reasons not necessarily in the client's best interest.

Four chapters of the bankruptcy code are available to individuals seeking protection from creditors. They are Chapters 7, 11, 12, and 13. Chapter 7 is commonly known as "straight bankruptcy," because it results in all dischargeable debts being discharged. An individual filing bankruptcy under Chapter 7 is required to submit all nonexempt assets to a trustee for cash liquidation and distribution to the creditors. All dischargeable debts are discharged if a creditor fails to file an objection within the time fixed by the court in the notice the court sends to the creditors when a Chapter 7 bankruptcy is filed.

Chapter 11 is another common form of bankruptcy. It is generally used for reorganizing a business, but in certain cases can be used by individuals. Next is Chapter 12. This chapter is specifically designed to aid the family farmer who, because of the special economics of running a family farm, has too much debt to qualify as a debtor under Chapter 13 and for whom Chapter 11, a business reorganization, is needlessly complicated and usually unworkable.

Finally, there is Chapter 13. This option is generally available to individuals with unsecured debts amounting to no more than $100,000 and whose secured debts are less than

When Bankruptcy is the Only Way Out

$350,000. This chapter basically establishes a repayment plan which must be approved by the court but does not require the approval of the individual's creditors.

Once you make the decision to file bankruptcy, a choice of appropriate chapter to use is your next decision. Most consumers should probably choose straight bankruptcy under Chapter 7. The majority of individuals filing bankruptcy have little or no nonexempt property for which they might claim protection under Chapter 13. Generally they will not have sufficient income in excess of their needs for living expenses which would allow them to negotiate a repayment plan with their creditors.

Because of these circumstances, most consumers generally obtain a quick and easy "fresh start" through Chapter 7. The most frequent decision is the discharge of most, if not all, of their debts.

Selecting the Right Chapter

Unless you are a family farmer or a person with significant assets or extremely large debts, then your bankruptcy options are simple. On the one hand, you can select Chapter 7 and face liquidation of any nonexempt assets you may own, or you can select Chapter 13 and face a prolonged period of repaying your debts.

We cannot advise you personally which course of action is best in your individual case. Only a competent, experienced attorney who has closely examined your circumstances can help you select the right chapter.

The information contained in the following chapters will help you evaluate your situation, especially the presence of nonexempt property which you may want to keep, and reach your own conclusion as to which chapter of the Bankruptcy Code will offer the relief you need.

A few questions you should ask yourself when evaluating your situation are

- Do I have nonexempt property I do not want to lose in a Chapter 7 liquidation?
- What are my chances of holding onto that property, especially if it was used to secure a debt, in a Chapter 13 case?
- Will I be able to commit myself to several years of a tight budget in which all my disposable income will be used to repay my debts in a Chapter 13 case?
- Do I want to resolve my financial problems quickly, or can I tolerate dragging them out over three or more years?
- Can I continue the required payments during the course of the plan without incurring any significant new obligations that may impact on my ability to carry out the plan?
- Am I concerned with what is perceived by some people as the "stigma" attached to "straight" bankruptcy? If so, should I consider only a repayment plan under Chapter 13?

With these questions in mind, and any others that might apply to your current situation, read the next four chapters carefully. Each describes a different chapter of bankruptcy and will help you select the chapter most appropriate for you.

Six

WHAT YOU SHOULD KNOW ABOUT CHAPTER 7 BANKRUPTCY

DECIDING IF CHAPTER 7 IS RIGHT FOR YOU

If your debts become completely unmanageable, they can usually be eliminated through a Chapter 7 filing. However, certain legal exemptions may allow you to keep your home and other possessions. Once you file your petition with the bankruptcy court, you are protected from most actions by your creditors by virtue of the "automatic stay" provision of the Bankruptcy Code.

Chapter 7 is a basic liquidation or straight bankruptcy. It is designed for individuals who are unable to pay their debts from their income and desire to make a fresh start. Under this chapter the debtor is permitted to retain certain property specified in federal and state laws. Later chapters and Appendix A will help you identify these exemptions. The debtor's remaining property is assigned to a court-appointed trustee who sells it and distributes the funds received from the sale to the creditors.

When the process is complete, all dischargeable debts are canceled, and the debtor no longer has the legal obliga-

You *Can* Go Bankrupt *Without* Going Broke

tion to pay the "discharged" debts included on the list of creditors filed with the bankruptcy petition.

When to Use Chapter 7

Chapter 7 bankruptcy is recommended when you do not own nonexempt property you wish to protect from seizure and sale. Also, if you lack the regular income required to finance a repayment program under one of the other chapters, Chapter 7 is the obvious choice.

Who Is Eligible for Chapter 7

Any person living in the United States, who does business, or owns property in this country, may file for a Chapter 7 bankruptcy. Despite what many people believe, it is not necessary that your debts have a greater dollar value than your assets in order to file; however, as a practical matter it is usually not wise to file unless this is true.

A married couple is usually best advised to file a joint bankruptcy, particularly if each owes one or more substantial dischargeable debts. Should only one file, creditors will usually seek to collect the full amount of their debts from the nonfiling spouse, even if he or she is unemployed, for example, a housewife whose husband has filed bankruptcy.

THE CHAPTER 7 FILING

Far too many people delay filing bankruptcy until creditors have inundated their lives. Only after they have suffered the embarrassment of garnished wages or been harassed by collection agencies will they think to turn to the bankruptcy court for protection.

When to File Chapter 7

Although you will not wish to wait until your overwhelming

Chapter 7 Bankruptcy

debts begin to take a psychological toll, several factors should be considered before filing. You may wish to delay filing if you expect to incur a sizable new debt. For example, if you or someone for whom you are legally responsible, such as a child, has been seriously ill and under expensive medical care, you will want to consider waiting to receive all the bills before you file, so they may be included. If you do not wait, you will not be able to discharge these new bills for at least another six years. It is important however, to avoid incurring these debts with fraudulent intent. For example, knowing in advance you are not going to pay them will label them nondischargeable debts.

Another reason to delay filing is if you expect to receive a large sum of money or valuable property within six months, such as an inheritance, divorce property settlement, or proceeds from a life insurance policy. Under the law, these types of properties must be surrendered to the trustee for distribution to your creditors.

What Is Filed

A Chapter 7 bankruptcy requires filing a petition accompanied by a listing of your assets and your debts, plus a statement describing your financial situation. This information is filed with the clerk of the bankruptcy court serving the region where you live. A married couple is permitted to file one petition including the foregoing information for both parties.

What the Court Fees Are

Individuals filing Chapter 7 bankruptcy are required to pay a filing fee to the court. At the time of this writing, the fee is $120. As a general rule you will have to pay this when you file your petition. Sometimes the court will allow this fee to be paid in as many as four installments. A married couple filing a joint petition is charged the same fee as an individual filing alone. Failure to pay the court fee could result in a delay in the discharge of your debts, or it may even result in having your petition dismissed.

THE CHAPTER 7 PROCESS

What the Bankruptcy Trustee Does

When a Chapter 7 bankruptcy filing is received by the clerk of the court, the case is assigned to a trustee. This is an individual appointed by a federal official known as a U.S. Trustee. The trustee is usually selected from a group of local attorneys who specialize in bankruptcy and has volunteered to act as trustee.

In return for a generally small fee representing a percentage of the value of your nonexempt assets, the trustee is responsible for collecting those nonexempt assets, selling those which are liquid—usually through an auction—and distributing the proceeds to the creditors.

How Creditors Are Notified

All creditors listed on the schedules accompanying your bankruptcy petition are notified by the court of your filing. This is done by the court clerk shortly after your petition is received. If your creditors are overly zealous and you prefer not to wait until the court clerk's notices are mailed, you can mail your own, or your attorney will do it for you.

The notification to creditors demands that all actions they may have taken, or plan on taking, against you must stop. This is called the "automatic stay" provision. The law requires that all creditor activities designed to collect on their accounts must be discontinued. This includes wage garnishments and even telephone calls to you demanding payment.

Chapter 7 Bankruptcy

Certain actions are not halted by a bankruptcy filing: some of them are criminal cases; those aimed at collecting debts for spousal support, child support, and maintenance; or those concerning property which is not part of the Chapter 7 estate, such as property you acquire after the filing.

The Meeting of Your Creditors

Roughly one month after your bankruptcy petition is filed, you will be required to make a court appearance. Your attorney will make this appearance with you to ensure your rights are protected. This appearance is usually referred to as a "341(a) meeting," because the procedure is mandated by Section 341(a) of the Bankruptcy Code.

Joining you and your attorney at this meeting will be the trustee assigned to your case and any creditors who wish to appear. The law forbids bankruptcy judges from attending these meetings; therefore, the trustee presides. This is done to preserve the independence of bankruptcy judges who may later have to resolve questions arising in the case.

Most creditors do not bother to attend these meetings unless there are unusual circumstances, such as a creditor claiming that a specific debt should not be discharged. In most courts these meetings are held on a specified day of the week, and debtors are usually surprised to find the courthouse halls crowded with bankruptcy filers and their attorneys.

Questions You Must Answer

During the 341(a) meeting you will be placed under oath and the trustee will ask a series of questions about your assets and the information contained in your filing. The disclosure is designed to determine if all your assets have been accounted for and if you have engaged in any suspicious or potentially illegal activities prior to the bankruptcy filing, such as transferring assets to avoid their seizure. Any creditors attending the meeting are also entitled to ask questions about your financial affairs and property.

Following are questions typically asked of debtors by bankruptcy trustees at the first meeting of creditors:

1. What are your full name and current address?
2. Do you own or rent your home?
3. What is your spouse's name?
4. When were you married?
5. Did you ever have another name?
6. Have you made any voluntary or involuntary transfers of real or personal property within the last year?
7. Are any of your debts from credit card use?
8. Is Schedule A-1 a complete list of your creditors having priority?
9. Is Schedule A-2 a complete list of your creditors having security?
10. Is Schedule A-3 a complete list of your unsecured creditors?
11. Is Schedule B-1 a complete list of all your real property?
12. Is Schedule B-2 a complete list of all your personal property?
13. Is Schedule B-3 a complete list of your other property?
14. Is Schedule B-4 a complete list of all property you claim as exempt?
15. Is the Summary of Assets and Debts a complete and accurate total of your property and debts?

These are usually followed by additional questions regarding previously owned real or personal property, recent payments made to creditors, and any potential windfall income expected in the near future, such as a tax refund or award from a lawsuit. Finally, there are questions about your current employment and the reason for your present financial

Chapter 7 Bankruptcy

situation. Unless there are unusual aspects about your case, the questions tend to be routine and easily answered to the trustee's satisfaction.

Although meeting creditors is theoretically an adversarial procedure, in practice there are rarely any disputes because most Chapter 7 filers have little or no nonexempt property and most creditors do not bother to attend. The average meeting takes less than fifteen minutes, and this will probably be the only time you will need to appear in court in relation to your bankruptcy filing.

The speed with which these procedures are handled often surprises an individual involved in a bankruptcy case. Most expect to have to spend countless hours in court during numerous appearances at which every aspect of their lives will be exposed to criticism and ridicule. Nothing could be farther from the truth. The procedure is generally routine, and most of the people involved are as anxious as you to get through it.

Asset and No-Asset Cases

If it appears that you have no money and no nonexempt assets which can be used to pay your debts, your creditors will be advised by the clerk of the bankruptcy court not to bother filing a claim unless they have reason to believe their debt is nondischargeable. If no objection is filed by a creditor, your case will move swiftly to a discharge of your debts.

If your case does involve nonexempt assets, your creditors have 90 days from the date of the meeting of creditors to file proof of their claims. The trustee will examine these claims and determine who is entitled to receive a portion of your assets. If any of the claims are objectionable, the trustee will file the necessary objection with the court so that the issue may be resolved by the bankruptcy judge. When all funds from the sale of nonexempt property have been distributed, the case is closed.

THE RESOLUTION OF YOUR FILING

How Your Debts Are Discharged

Provided there are no complications such as a challenge to specific debts included in the bankruptcy filing, or a dispute as to the exemption of a particular piece of property, or an objection to your bankruptcy filing by the trustee assigned to your case, in approximately four months you will receive a "discharge." This means you are no longer obligated to pay many of the unsecured debts the trustee was unable to pay from your assets. All of the unsecured debts included with your filing which have not been successfully challenged by your creditors are no longer enforceable—they are "discharged." Creditors whose unsecured debts have been discharged can no longer take collection action against you for these particular debts.

What Happens After the Discharge

Although a bankruptcy filing, just as any other court case, is public record, don't expect your local newspaper to take note of your bankruptcy, unless you are a local celebrity. The discharge of your debts means you have an opportunity to start over again. It will be a long, difficult struggle to establish new credit and to break any bad habits that may have helped lead you into the financial problems that ended in bankruptcy. In the final chapter of this book, we offer some advice on how you can take advantage of this fresh start the Bankruptcy Code has given you.

Why Your Case Could Be Dismissed

The court may dismiss your filing for a number of reasons. It

Chapter 7 Bankruptcy

is your attorney's responsibility to help you avoid dismissal by ensuring you are aware of actions which might lead to such a decision.

The most common reasons for a dismissal include

1. failure, on your part, to cooperate with the trustee who has been appointed to handle your case in the lawful execution of the trustee's duties.
2. the court's determination that granting you relief of your debts will result in substantial abuse of the provisions of Chapter 7. This usually applies only to high-income debtors who are probably capable of repaying their debts under another chapter.
3. committing fraud during the bankruptcy proceedings, such as providing false information concerning your assets or your income.
4. failure to obey a lawful order of the court or to adhere to the procedures of the court, including filing the proper papers, attending the meeting of creditors, and attending and testifying at any hearings resulting from objections filed by creditors.

It is vitally important that you be completely honest with your attorney to ensure you are competently protected from committing an act that could result in the dismissal of your filing. This is especially true in cases of bankruptcy fraud, which under federal criminal law is a felony that could result in your prosecution.

How to Deal with Secured Creditors

Since bankruptcy does not provide for the discharge of debts secured by personal or real property, these matters are treated differently. The most common items used as collateral are large-ticket items purchased on credit provided by the seller, such as automobiles, furniture, and major appliances. You have three options available when dealing with secured creditors:

1. You can surrender the item used as collateral to obtain the loan.
2. You can continue to make the payments on the secured loan.
3. You can redeem the item used as collateral by paying the creditor its full market value.

If you wish to retain ownership of secured items, you are required to take positive action during the bankruptcy proceedings. Few individuals filing straight bankruptcy have the cash on hand, or the ability to raise enough cash, to use option 3 and redeem the items they used as collateral. If you have sufficient income to permit you to continue making payments on the secured items, option 2 is a viable solution.

Why You Should Refuse to Sign a Reaffirmation Agreement
In most cases secured creditors are happy to allow you to keep the collateral if you continue to make payments. These secured creditors may request that you sign a legal and enforceable agreement that promises you will repay the full amount outstanding on a timely basis. This agreement is called a "reaffirmation agreement" because in it you declare that the debt will be paid regardless of the pending bankruptcy. The agreement is signed by you and the creditor and is filed with the bankruptcy court.

This agreement binds you to pay the debt or surrender the collateral. In return, the creditor promises that so long as you make the payments it will not attempt to repossess the property. Most secured creditors are happy to execute a reaffirmation agreement because, with the notable exception of car dealers, they are not in the business of selling used

Chapter 7 Bankruptcy

items and prefer to avoid the expense involved in repossessing used merchandise.

To become effective under the law, a reaffirmation agreement must meet the following criteria:

1. It must be agreed to and signed by both debtor and creditor before the bankruptcy discharge is granted.
2. The debtor retains the right to cancel the agreement at any time before the discharge is granted or within sixty days of the date the agreement is filed with the court, whichever is later. The agreement must contain a clear statement informing the debtor of this right to cancel.
3. The court must warn the debtor of the potential consequences of the reaffirmation and what could happen if the debtor defaults on the agreement.
4. The attorney who negotiated the agreement for the debtor must certify that the agreement does not place an undue hardship on the client. If there was no debtor's attorney involved in negotiating the agreement, the court must ensure the agreement is in the debtor's best interests and places no undue hardship on the debtor.

It should be noted, however, that a person filing bankruptcy who is able to continue making regular payments to secured creditors can simply do so without any written agreement, unless the secured creditor insists on the execution of a formal reaffirmation agreement. There is little or no necessity to reaffirm a legal obligation if you plan to meet the original obligation.

Courts have ruled that secured property cannot be repossessed if the payments are maintained on schedule. Moreover, as we have already said, few creditors are genuinely interested in assuming the cost and bother of repossessing their merchandise if they believe they will continue getting paid. After all, what is the department store going to do with your used sofa or used washing machine? Even automobile dealers would rather gamble on your continued payments than repossess a car they will have to sell at a price that will be substantially less than what you owe and have to pay repossession costs and sales commissions when it is finally sold.

Reaffirmation agreements are generally not in the best interest of individuals filing Chapter 7 bankruptcy. When a secured creditor threatens repossession if you do not enter into a reaffirmation agreement, you might be better off telling the creditor you intend to continue meeting your obligation to it. Most creditors will not pursue a co-debtor if the payments are made, and few will want the merchandise back if you are paying for it.

A recent study of bankruptcy law and practices found that many debtors continued to pay their secured creditors after bankruptcy without a formal agreement. Most creditors acquiesced to this and took no action against the debtors.

Seven

WHAT YOU SHOULD KNOW ABOUT CHAPTER 11 BANKRUPTCY

DECIDING IF CHAPTER 11 IS RIGHT FOR YOU

Of the remaining relevant chapters in the Bankruptcy Code, Chapter 12 was written especially for family farmers, and Chapter 13 is for debtors who desire to repay their debts and are able to do so over a specified period of time. Neither discharges your debts completely, as does Chapter 7, but they provide an opportunity to "reorganize" your financial affairs and eventually repay the money you owe, while usually preventing seizure of nonexempt property by creditors.

Who Is Eligible for Chapter 11

Eligibility to file under Chapter 13 is limited, among other factors, to individuals whose unsecured debts are less than $100,000 and secured debts are less than $350,000. Individuals with debt exceeding these limits may file under Chapter 11. This better known reorganization chapter is available to individuals, corporations, and partnerships. It is the chapter used most frequently when companies reorganize or individuals with large amounts of cash or nonexempt holdings seek protection from creditors.

The Advantages of Chapter 11

Like Chapter 13, which we will discuss later, Chapter 11 involves developing a plan to pay creditors rather than liquidating the debtor's holdings and discharging all dischargeable debts. A major advantage Chapter 11 has over Chapter 13, aside from having no limit on debt, is that it is possible to file a Chapter 11 case without the appointment of a trustee. This means you can exercise some of the power, with certain exceptions, that is vested in the trustee under a Chapter 13 filing.

Another advantage of a Chapter 11 filing is that it buys time. A financially troubled company or debtor can use a Chapter 11 action to hold off creditors in anticipation of resolving the financial problems through other means. A Chapter 13 filing must include the plan defining how the debtor will repay the debts. It must be filed no later than 15 days after the petition. A Chapter 11 filing entitles the debtor to an initial period of 120 days before a payment plan must be submitted. This period may be extended. The debtor in a Chapter 11 case also has greater control and flexibility in developing the "plan of reorganization."

Who Chapter 11 Helps

Although Chapter 11 is basically structured to serve businesses, individual consumers are also eligible to use it. As a practical matter, an individual filing under Chapter 11 should have something to reorganize, rehabilitate, or liquidate before Chapter 11 relief can be granted. It is especially useful for individuals with large state or federal tax obligations because an extended period of time may be obtained for the repayment of the taxes.

Chapter 11 Bankruptcy

THE CHAPTER 11 PROCESS

A Chapter 11 case begins with the filings of a petition requesting the bankruptcy court to grant the debtor relief under this chapter of the Bankruptcy Code. Additional documents required include detailed schedules of assets and liabilities, a statement of the debtor's financial affairs, and related items. If these documents are not prepared at the time of filing, they must be submitted to the court within 15 days. At the time of filing, the fee is paid, or the court clerk may approve a plan to allow the fee to be paid in installments.

How Court Fees Are Set

Because cases involving large sums of money or valuable assets are often complex, a Chapter 11 filing is more expensive. When the petition is filed, it must be accompanied by a filing fee of $500. In addition, the U.S. trustee is paid a quarterly fee during the period in which a payment plan is being developed, until one is approved. The amount of this quarterly fee is dependent on the amount of disbursements made by the debtor and can range from $150 to as much as $3,000 each quarter.

Developing a Payment Plan

Having filed the appropriate documents, a debtor has an initial 120-day period, which may be extended, in which to prepare and submit a payment plan. During this period an automatic stay is in effect, preventing all creditors from taking any action to collect on the filer's debts. The stay remains in effect until a plan has been accepted and confirmed by the court. This procedure may take up to twelve months or longer, depending on the size and complexity of the debtor's case.

Along with a plan to repay creditors, the debtor must also file a disclosure statement which informs the creditors of the debtor's financial condition and future plans. The court can approve or disapprove the disclosure statement after receiving comments from creditors and the U.S. trustee's office. Once approved, it is disseminated to the creditors, along with a copy of the payment plan. The creditors will now vote whether to accept or reject the plan.

How Your Plan Is Approved

Each creditor is mailed a disclosure statement and plan along with a ballot on which to vote. The court sets a deadline for the return of all ballots. The only creditors eligible to vote in this process are those classified as "impaired." This means any creditor who will not receive the full amount of money owed by the debtor, under the plan developed by the debtor, can vote. Any creditor who will receive the full amount owed is not entitled to a vote.

If the plan is accepted by a majority, in number, of the eligible voters, and two-thirds of those actually casting a vote, a confirmation hearing is held to allow the court to give its approval. Once confirmed by the court, the plan takes effect immediately. Most plans are projected over three to five years, during which creditors will receive the approved payments.

As mentioned earlier, Chapter 11 is designed especially for businesses seeking to reorganize so they can continue operating while trying to settle their debts. It is also a viable alternative to Chapter 13 repayment plans for individuals with large tax debts, valuable assets, or debts running at or above $100,000 for unsecured debts or $350,000 for secured debts.

The decision as to which chapter to file, if any, should

Chapter 11 Bankruptcy

be made in consultation with an experienced attorney who specializes in personal bankruptcy. The intricacies of the applicable laws and the practices of the local bankruptcy court demand expertise before deciding on a course of action.

Eight

WHAT YOU SHOULD KNOW ABOUT CHAPTER 12 BANKRUPTCY

DECIDING IF CHAPTER 12 IS RIGHT FOR YOU

In 1986, responding to the widely publicized plight of American farm families, Congress created a sort of super Chapter 13 which became the new Chapter 12 of the Bankruptcy Code. Many family farmers became overextended during the 1970s and early 1980s, by purchasing expensive equipment and expanding their land holdings. The overall debt of family farms reached an all-time high when the economy took a sharp downturn and caught many farmers in a severe crunch.

Unable to meet their debts, many farmers were forced to resort to Chapter 7 bankruptcies, which resulted in the loss of their farms. Many had debts exceeding the limitations authorized under Chapter 13, even though their incomes would have permitted them to file under that chapter. Under Chapter 12 farmers are offered an alternative which allows them to keep their farms while developing a plan to repay their debts.

If you are a farmer with debts that exceed the limits of Chapter 13, then Chapter 12 is probably your best alternative.

Chapter 12 Bankruptcy

Who Is Eligible for Chapter 12

Chapter 12 identifies an eligible "family farmer" as a family or individual owning and operating a farm with a regular annual income sufficiently stable to make payments under a repayment plan which meets the following criteria:

1. The farmer must have no more than $1.5 million total debt, both secured and unsecured.
2. Not less that 80 percent of the farmer's debts must arise directly from the farming operation, excluding the mortgage on the family residence.
3. At least 50 percent of the previous tax year's gross income of the farmer and spouse, if any, must come from the operation of the farm.

The Advantages of Chapter 12

Family farmers meeting the eligibility requirements of Chapter 12 will find this procedure less complicated than Chapter 11, under which most farmers were previously forced to file if their debt exceeded the limits of Chapter 13 and if they didn't want to lose everything in a Chapter 7 straight bankruptcy. Usually Chapter 12 is also less time consuming, less expensive, and more workable than a Chapter 11 filing.

Perhaps the most significant advantage a Chapter 12 filing holds for the working farmer is that it permits a farmer who is unable to repay debt to "write down" secured debts to the current value of the land. This amounts to paying the creditor on what is essentially an adjusted mortgage based on the actual value of the farm.

THE CHAPTER 12 PROCESS

How Co-signers Are Protected

An important difference between Chapter 12 and Chapters 7

and 11 of the Bankruptcy Code appears in the automatic stay provisions. Under Chapters 7 and 11 a creditor must stop all action against a debtor who has filed for bankruptcy, but can initiate, or continue, action against any nonfiling co-signers of the debts from which relief is being sought. Similar to Chapter 13, when a family farmer files under Chapter 12, the automatic stay is extended to co-signers as well as to the filer.

Your Repayment Period

Unless the court grants an extension of the period during which the farmer must repay the debts, the repayment must be made in three years. The court, however, has the authority to extend this to a maximum of five years.

How Creditors Are Treated

Secured creditors have the right to accept a repayment plan or decline to participate and receive the property used as collateral. Unsecured creditors are not required to vote on acceptance of the plan, but they are protected by a clause known as the "best interest" test. Under this test creditors are guaranteed to receive at least the same amount under the repayment plan as they would receive had the farmer filed a Chapter 7 bankruptcy case.

Nine

WHAT YOU SHOULD KNOW ABOUT CHAPTER 13 BANKRUPTCY

DECIDING IF CHAPTER 13 IS RIGHT FOR YOU

Chapter 13 of the Bankruptcy Code is designed for use as a flexible vehicle under which overwhelming debts can be repaid without losing property. It is available to an individual and married couples filing together, but not to a corporation or most other business entities. A Chapter 13 filing is also usually faster and less costly than is a Chapter 11 filing.

You must keep in mind that a Chapter 13 filing does not relieve you of your debts in the same way as does a Chapter 7 filing, but adjusts the conditions under which you must pay them.

When to Use Chapter 13

The Chapter 13 alternative to straight bankruptcy offers unique advantages to debtors who feel they can repay some part, or in certain circumstances, where desirable or required, all of their debts.

Chapter 13 is probably the best option if your situation fits into one of the following categories:

1. You own nonexempt assets with a total value which equals or exceeds the amount you owe, but you want to keep them. These might include assets such as stocks, bonds, real estate, or stamp or coin collections, whose current market value is expected to climb appreciably in the near future. No one wants to sell undervalued property to repay debts which could be better repaid when the market for those assets improves. If you file under Chapter 13, and are able to maintain the approved payment schedule, you can always sell the property later at a better price and complete your payment schedule in a lump sum and obtain your Chapter 13 discharge.
2. You received a Chapter 7 discharge in the previous six years and are therefore barred from filing Chapter 7 again, and thus must turn to Chapter 13 for help.
3. Your debts are the result of purchases of items on which you owe substantially less than their current value, such as a car. Under Chapter 7 these assets might be returned to the creditors, and you could lose the equity you have built up in them since their purchase.
4. You have a co-signer on one or more debts whom you want to protect from the creditors. A repayment schedule under Chapter 13 will allow you to do this. However, if you file a straight Chapter 7 bankruptcy, the creditors are entitled to take action against the co-signer for collection.
5. You gave false information on a credit application, or otherwise committed fraud in obtaining credit, and there is reason to believe at least one creditor is aware of your actions. In these circumstances that creditor can file a complaint to determine the dischargeability of that debt in your Chapter 7 case. This could result in that debt being found to be nondischargeable. This would not happen in a Chapter 13 filing.

Chapter 13 Bankruptcy

One of the most common reasons for selecting Chapter 13 is the presence of secured creditors whose claims cannot be handled satisfactorily in another way. The couple in the following example are somewhat representative of a large portion of the people who file under Chapter 13 each year.

> William and Edna Head were facing serious financial difficulties. They had been telling themselves they would be able to find a way out before the situation got worse, but they had to face reality when the bank which held their car loan informed them the car was going to be repossessed as a result of nonpayment. In what they thought of as an act of final desperation, the Heads visited an attorney who specialized in bankruptcy cases. The attorney reviewed the Heads' situation and realized Mr. Head would probably lose his job if he lost the car. Taking this and other factors into account, the attorney recommended the Heads file for bankruptcy under Chapter 13. The filing immediately halted all legal action against the Heads, including the threatened repossession of their car.

No legal action can prevent the repossession of an item as quickly or effectively as a Chapter 13 filing. Whether it is your automobile, home, or furniture, when your creditors threaten foreclosure or repossession, that may be a clear signal to seriously consider filing a Chapter 13 petition to stop all actions against you until you can work out a reasonable plan to repay your creditors.

The Advantages of Chapter 13

Chapter 13 offers debtors a wide range of advantages over a straight bankruptcy when a Chapter 7 is a serious option. The advantages over doing nothing to ward off your creditors are tremendous. These advantages are:

You *Can* Go Bankrupt *Without* Going Broke

1. With certain exceptions such as child support and spousal support, Chapter 13 will allow more debts to be discharged than will a Chapter 7 filing, including some which are considered nondischargeable in a Chapter 7 case.
2. Assets which are otherwise considered nonexempt in a Chapter 7 filing can be protected from seizure in a Chapter 13 case.
3. Under certain circumstances, a "hardship discharge" can be granted a Chapter 13 filer before the debts have been repaid.
4. The automatic stay of actions by creditors which is afforded by any bankruptcy filing extends to any co-signers of the debts included in a Chapter 13 bankruptcy filing.
5. A person filing Chapter 13 generally remains in possession of all property. You may continue to use personal property which has a lien against it while the creditor's claim is being paid off under the plan.
6. If, in the middle of your bankruptcy case, your situation changes and you want to drop the filing, you can do so if you filed Chapter 13; but if you filed a Chapter 7 case, the court must approve dismissing the case.
7. Your credit standing may receive greater protection when you file a Chapter 13 rather than a Chapter 7 case.

A vital benefit derived from a Chapter 13 filing is that under the proper circumstances, an unsecured creditor is forced to accept a payment plan which pays only a portion of the money owed, and more importantly, creditors can be prevented from foreclosing or placing liens on your property.

The Disadvantages of Chapter 13

While unsecured creditors may be compelled to accept a payment plan for less than the full amount due them, in most

Chapter 13 Bankruptcy

situations secured creditors cannot be forced to do so. Most secured creditors are dealt with separately. A Chapter 13 plan depends on the debtor maintaining a stable and constant income. The plan may fail if the debtor's income is interrupted by a layoff or injury or some other contingency that reduces or eliminates the income. Compared to Chapter 7 cases, Chapter 13 cases last much longer and are more expensive. Unlike a Chapter 7 filing, when you file a Chapter 13, your employer may sometimes need to be informed of your situation.

Finally, although your credit standing may be better protected, the fact that you filed a Chapter 13 petition will be reflected in credit reports and may deter some creditors from granting you new credit. This decision depends on the policy of the companies from which you seek credit.

Who Is Eligible for Chapter 13

Chapter 13 is available to any individual meeting the criteria in the list that follows. It is open to individuals, married couples filing a joint petition, and owners of small businesses operating as sole proprietorships, but not to partnerships or corporations. To qualify for a Chapter 13 filing, debtors must meet the following guidelines:

1. They must reside in, do business in, or own property in the United States.
2. They must have a regular source of income that is sufficient enough to allow participation in what will ultimately be an approved repayment plan.
3. Their unsecured debts must be less than $100,000.
4. Their secured debts must be less than $350,000.
5. They may not be a stockbroker or commodity broker.
6. They were not debtors in another bankruptcy case that was dismissed for certain technical reasons during the previous 180 days.

If a married couple files a joint petition, only one party is required to meet the criteria of having a regular income, but the debt limits apply to both parties. If a husband has $80,000 in unsecured debts, and his wife has $55,000 in unsecured debts, the total unsecured debts for the filing would be $135,000, thus making them ineligible to file a joint petition. A couple in this situation might have to file separate petitions, depending on the circumstances, particularly if they co-signed for each other.

THE CHAPTER 13 FILING

A Chapter 13 filer is someone who expects to repay all or part of outstanding debts if allowed to restructure the present payment arrangement. Ideally, this means lower payments stretched over a longer period of time. In a Chapter 13 case you must prepare and submit to the court a plan for the payment of your debts, as well as a schedule of your assets and liabilities, and a statement of your financial affairs.

About Your Payment Plan

Your plan may include secured and unsecured debts. You are required to include all debts in your plan. The plan need not call for all unsecured creditors receiving the full amount of money owed them. You will be required to make payments to a trustee who in turn will disburse the money to the creditors as described in the plan. Payments to the trustee must begin thirty days after filing the plan, even if it has not yet been approved by the court.

Your Filing Costs

Individuals filing a Chapter 13 case are required to pay a filing fee to the clerk of the bankruptcy court. At the time of this writing, the fee is $120. Generally, this fee is payable

            Chapter 13 Bankruptcy

when your petition is filed, although in some cases the court will permit the fee to be paid in as many as four installments. A married couple is charged the same amount when filing a joint petition. Because a court-appointed trustee will handle the payments under your plan, additional costs may accrue for this service.

THE CHAPTER 13 PROCESS

When the clerk of the court receives a Chapter 13 bankruptcy filing, a Chapter 13 trustee is appointed to administer the case. Under the jurisdiction of a federal official known as the U.S. trustee, Chapter 13 trustees are selected from a group of local attorneys who specialize in bankruptcy and have volunteered to act as trustees.

What the Bankruptcy Trustee Does

Unlike a Chapter 7 filing where the trustee's duties may be limited by the existence of nonexempt property and other assets, the trustee in a Chapter 13 case acts as a disbursing agent. The trustee collects the amount of money stipulated in the plan and disburses it directly to the creditors. For this service, the trustee receives 10 percent of all payments made. Therefore, if your payments total $8,000 under a court-approved plan, $800 of that money is paid to the trustee.

Your Employer May Be Notified

Depending on the circumstances of your case and the policy of the local federal bankruptcy court, your employer may be notified of your filing. Under some circumstances your employer may be required to make payments to the trustee on your behalf, by deducting the money from your salary. Even if this is not done, the trustee may contact your employer to verify your employment and your income. If you can provide the evidence in some other way, and there are compelling reasons not to inform your employer, exceptions can be made.

How Creditors Are Notified

All creditors listed on the schedules accompanying your bankruptcy petition are notified by the court of your filing. This is done by the court clerk a short time after your petition is filed. If your creditors are threatening legal action and you do not choose to wait for the court clerk to notify them, your attorney may do so. You may also do the same as a courtesy to family members and friends who are creditors.

This notification also requires that all actions taken or contemplated against you must stop. This includes any actions against co-signers as well. The law insists that all creditor activities designed to collect debts must be discontinued, including wage garnishments, and even harassing telephone calls demanding payment.

How a Payment Plan Is Established

With the help of your attorney, you are responsible for drawing up a plan which repays all or part of your unsecured debts. Generally the law limits the payment period to three years, although the court has the authority to extend it to as many as five years.

Before the plan can take effect, it must be approved by the court. To gain approval, a plan must meet the following standards:

1. It must comply with the legal requirements of the Bankruptcy Code.
2. You must have paid all required fees and charges.

Chapter 13 Bankruptcy

3. The bankruptcy judge has determined the plan was proposed in good faith.
4. Each unsecured creditor will receive at least as much money as it would have had you filed Chapter 7 bankruptcy and your nonexempt assets were liquidated and used to pay your debts.
5. You appear able to meet the payments required by the plan.
6. All of your disposable income has been committed to making payments as stated in the plan. Disposable income is defined as all income in excess of what you require for the support of yourself and your dependents.
7. All secured debts have been addressed as prescribed by law (see "How Secured Creditors Are Treated" later).

What Happens When Your Creditors Meet

Approximately one to two months after filing your petition, you will be required to attend a meeting of your creditors. This will be the first of what is normally only two appearances you will be required to make. Either the trustee administering your case or the court clerk will preside over the meeting.

Any creditors who so desire may attend this meeting. In most cases they do not. They will have the right to ask you questions concerning your financial affairs and your proposed repayment plan. Creditors have up to ninety days after the meeting to file a claim to ensure they are included in the payment plan. An unsecured creditor who fails to file such a claim within that period is barred from doing so later.

You have the right to challenge any claims filed by the creditors. If there are any disputes over the plan, they are usually resolved at the meeting or soon after by the bankruptcy judge if necessary.

You *Can* Go Bankrupt *Without* Going Broke

Your Confirmation Hearing

Approximately three months after the creditor's meeting you will be required to appear again—at what is called a confirmation hearing. At this time the bankruptcy judge determines whether the payment plan is feasible and if it meets Bankruptcy Code standards. Creditors have the right to appear at this hearing and object to the confirmation. The most common objections by creditors are that they will receive less money under the plan than had you filed a Chapter 7 straight bankruptcy and that the plan does not include all of your disposable income for payment of your debts. These objections are usually settled at the hearing.

Once the court approves the plan, the trustee begins the prescribed payments to the creditors from the money already paid over by you pursuant to your plan.

If Your Plan Is Not Confirmed

The court may refuse to confirm the plan if it does not meet the requirements of the Bankruptcy Code. If this happens, the money already deposited with the trustee is returned, less the trustee's fee. The plan may then be modified to meet these requirements, if that is possible. Often a plan is not approved because the judge finds the payments stipulated by the plan are overly ambitious and beyond the debtor's ability to pay on a regular basis.

If the plan can be modified to meet the requirements, it may be resubmitted to the court for approval. If it cannot be modified so that it can be approved, you may dismiss the case or convert it to a Chapter 7 case.

THE CHAPTER 13 DISCHARGE

When the payment plan is completed, the court will grant what is called a Section 1328(a) discharge. This means you

Chapter 13 Bankruptcy

no longer have to pay any debts which were included in the plan, even if the amount paid through the plan is less than the amount originally owed. Creditors who were provided for in your plan, either in the full amount owed or in part, cannot take any action against you to collect the remaining debt.

Included in this discharge are some debts that would be considered nondischargeable in a Chapter 7 case, such as debts incurred through fraud, embezzlement, larceny, and willful or malicious injury. This is the broadest type of discharge and is based on the individual's willingness to undergo the strict discipline of a three-year, or even five-year, payment plan that takes all disposable income.

Not included in this discharge are

1. debts not included in the plan
2. debts for alimony, maintenance, or child support
3. debts whose last payment is due after the date of the final payment under the plan
4. debts incurred while the plan was in effect

How Secured Creditors Are Treated

Secured creditors have several options from which to select a course of action when a debtor files a Chapter 13 case. Before examining these options, it is important to understand the rights of a secured creditor.

Secured creditors can

1. accept the plan as it is proposed or modified
2. retain their liens on the collateral
3. receive the value of their allowed claims
4. have the collateral returned if option 3 is not applicable
5. make a separate arrangement with the debtor outside of the plan

You *Can* Go Bankrupt *Without* Going Broke

What to Do If Your Plan Fails

If at any time during the payment period you are temporarily unable to meet the payments stipulated in the plan, for reasons such as injury or being temporarily out of work, the plan can usually be modified to enable you to continue making payments when you are once again able to do so.

If you are no longer able to make the required payments in the foreseeable future, three options are available:

1. You may convert the case to a Chapter 7 bankruptcy.
2. You may have the case dismissed.
3. You may have the debts discharged under a "hardship discharge."

When to Request a Hardship Discharge

A debtor making payments under a Chapter 13 plan who can no longer make payments for reasons beyond the debtor's control and through no fault of his or her own can request a "hardship discharge," provided the creditors have received at least a sum equal to the amount they would have received in a Chapter 7 case and a modification of the payment plan is shown to be impractical. Illness or injury which precludes employment with income sufficient to fund even a modified plan is usually the reason for a "hardship discharge." This discharge does not include

1. secured debts, such as mortgages or liens
2. unsecured debts that were not included in the plan
3. unsecured debts whose last payments are due after the date of the final payment under the plan
4. debts incurred while the plan was in effect
5. all debts considered nondischargeable in a Chapter 7 case

Ten

YOUR EXEMPTIONS: FROM ALABAMA TO WYOMING

Each of the 50 states has established its own laws governing the protection of assets when an individual files for bankruptcy and the percentage of each type of asset that is protected from seizure. Anyone planning to file bankruptcy should review the exemptions permitted by the state in which he or she resides. If the level of exemptions is not satisfactory, a review of other states might lead to the consideration to relocate. For some people facing bankruptcy, moving to another state is impractical, but for many others, such a move is not only practical, but could result in substantial savings through greater exemptions. The possibility of such a move should be contemplated as early as possible when bankruptcy looms on the horizon.

The following serves as a guide to those readers anticipating personal bankruptcy. By reviewing the information in this and the following chapter, you will be better prepared to protect more assets from creditors. As a rule, federal and state benefit payments are exempt, as are most retirement plans for public employees.

This chapter contains information on all assets except

You *Can* Go Bankrupt *Without* Going Broke

your house, condo, co-op, mobile home, and land. These are treated separately in the following chapter. Exemptions available under federal laws are permitted in some states. A review of which states allow federal exemptions and what those exemptions are can be found in Appendix A.

In the "Wages" sections of the following guide, reference is usually made to the minimum hourly wage. The current minimum hourly wage is $3.50, so a state such as Alabama that exempts thirty times the federal minimum hourly wage per week therefore exempts $3.50 × 30, or $105 per week.

ALABAMA

Wages: Seventy-five percent of all wages, salaries, and compensation for personal services, or thirty times the federal minimum hourly wage per week, whichever is greater, is exempt.

Disability Insurance: A maximum of $250 per month is exempted from the proceeds or avails of disability insurance payments. The same amount is exempted from annuity payments.

All Others: All of the following are 100 percent exempt: burial plots; a seat or pew in a house of worship; clothing; family portraits and pictures; books; most life insurance proceeds; growing or ungathered crops; payments for public assistance, worker's compensation benefits, unemployment compensation benefits, teacher retirement system benefits, fraternal benefit society benefits, state employee retirement system benefits, peace officer retirement and disability benefits, and Vietnam war POW benefits; and specific property held by a business partnership. There is also a $3,000 exemption that can be applied to any personal property not otherwise exempted.

Your Exemptions

ALASKA

Wages: The sole wage earner in a household can exempt $550 per week. Others can exempt up to $350 per week.

Motor Vehicle: There is a maximum $3,000 exemption for one motor vehicle, provided its total value does not exceed $20,000. Any value over $20,000 is considered nonexempt and must be paid.

Limited Exemptions: All the following have limits set on the amount that is exempt: personal jewelry, $1,000; tools of trade and professional books, $2,800; pets, $1,000; and household goods, wearing apparel, personal books, musical instruments, family portraits and heirlooms, $3,000 aggregate value.

All Others: All the following are 100 percent exempt: burial plots; assets and benefits of retirement plans; interest in specific partnership property; building materials; life insurance; health aids; crime victim reparation awards; longevity bonuses; liquor licenses; and payments for state disability benefits, unemployment benefits, teacher and public employee retirement benefits, child support payments, public assistance benefits, worker's compensation benefits, fraternal benefit society benefits, and medical benefits.

ARIZONA

Wages: Seventy-five percent of disposable income resulting from wages, salaries, and pension and retirement payments, or thirty times the federal minimum hourly wage per week, whichever is greater, is exempt.

Motor Vehicle: A disabled debtor is entitled to a $4,000 exemption for a motor vehicle; otherwise, the maximum exemption is $1,500.

You *Can* Go Bankrupt *Without* Going Broke

Limited Exemptions: A total of $4,000 in exemptions can be taken for the following household items: one kitchen table; one dining room table; four chairs for each (more if required); one living room couch; one living room chair plus one more per dependent; three living room coffee and end tables; three living room lamps; one living room carpet or rug; two beds plus one more per dependent; one bed table, dresser, and lamp per bed; bedding for each bed; pictures, oil paintings, and drawings made by debtor; family portraits and frames; one television; one radio; one stove; one refrigerator; one washing machine; one clothes dryer; and one vacuum cleaner. Other limited exemptions include wearing apparel, $500; musical instruments, $250; domestic pets, horses, milk cows, and poultry, $500; engagement and wedding rings, $1,000; books, $250; watch, $100; bank account, $150; tools and other items needed in the profession of the debtor or spouse, $2,500; machinery, utensils, feed, grain, seed, and animals of a farmer, $1,500; and life insurance proceeds payable to surviving spouse or child, $20,000. A total of $500 is exempted for one typewriter; one bicycle; one sewing machine; a family Bible; a cemetery plot; and one rifle, shotgun, or pistol.

All Others: All the following are 100 percent exempt: food, fuel, and provisions for six months; wheelchair and prescribed health aids; earnings of minor child; health, accident, and disability benefits; insurance proceeds for damaged or destroyed exempt property; damages awarded for wrongful levy or execution; arms, uniforms, and accouterments required by law; interest in specific partnership property; and payments for public assistance, unemployment compensation benefits, worker's compensation benefits, fraternal benefit society benefits, firefighters' relief and pension benefits, police pension benefits, teacher retirement benefits, and state employee retirement benefits.

Your Exemptions

ARKANSAS

Wages: Earned but unpaid wages due for sixty days receive an exemption of $25 per week.

Motor Vehicle: A maximum of a $1,200 exemption is permitted for one motor vehicle.

Limited Exemptions: A total of $750 in exemptions may be taken for tools or books used in the profession of the debtor or a dependent of the debtor. Up to $20,000 in contributions made to an IRA account more than one year before filing is exempt. In addition, a married or head of household debtor can exempt up to $500 of personal items of any nature. For all others, this assignable exemption is $200.

All Others: The following are 100 percent exempt: burial plots; payments for health, life, accident, or disability insurance; wearing apparel for the debtor's entire family; payments for public assistance, worker's compensation benefits, unemployment compensation benefits, fraternal benefit society benefits, group life insurance benefits, teacher and state police retirement benefits, disability insurance benefits, and fire and police pension and relief benefits; and the value of wedding bands, including diamonds of ½ carat or less.

CALIFORNIA

California has two sets of exemptions from which to choose. A married couple filing a joint bankruptcy petition must select from option 1 or option 2, but may not use both. The same is true of a single person filing a bankruptcy petition. In most cases a married person filing a single petition must use the exemptions in option 1. A married person might choose to file a single petition if all debts were incurred by that person, thus avoiding having to include the spouse in the bankruptcy.

You *Can* Go Bankrupt *Without* Going Broke

Option 1

Wages: Seventy-five percent of all wages and other income, such as interest paid on deposit accounts, is exempt in this option when paid within thirty days of the filing.

Motor Vehicle: Up to $1,200 of equity in any number of motor vehicles is exempt.

Limited Exemptions: A total of $2,500 in exemptions can be taken for tools, books, and equipment required for use in a trade or business by the debtor. This can be doubled if the spouse requires tools and so on for trade or business. Other limited exemptions include $2,500 for jewelry, family heirlooms, and paintings; $1,000 in residential building materials; a maximum of $1,000 in a prison inmate's trust account. Bank accounts used for direct deposit of social security funds receive a $750 exemption for two or more payees and $500 for a single payee. All social security funds in the account are exempt. There is a $4,000 exemption each for the debtor and spouse on the aggregate loan values of unmatured life insurance policies. The proceeds on matured life insurance policies are exempt to an amount reasonably necessary to support the debtor and all dependents. A similar determination is made on self-employed retirement plan benefits.

All Others: Unlimited exemptions are granted on the following: all necessary personal household furnishings, provisions, appliances, wearing apparel, and other personal effects of all family members; burial plots for debtor and spouse; health aids and orthopedic or prosthetic devices; specific partnership property; personal injury and wrongful death claims; and payments for the following: public assistance benefits, unemployment compensation benefits, worker's compensation benefits, relocation benefits, welfare and fraternal bene-

Your Exemptions

fit society benefits, health and disability insurance benefits, and student financial aid from a college or university.

Option 2

Wages: There is no exemption for wages and other income under this option.

Motor Vehicle: A maximum of $1,200 in exemption can be taken for one motor vehicle.

Limited Exemptions: A maximum of $4,000 in total value, with a limit of $200 per item of exemption can be taken on household furnishings, wearing apparel, appliances, books, musical instruments, crops, and animals, if used personally by the debtor or the debtor's dependents. Other limited exemptions include up to $500 in personal or household jewelry; $750 worth of tools, books, and equipment used in trade or business by the debtor or debtor's dependent; unmatured life insurance loan value to $4,000; and up to $7,500 in payments for personal bodily injury. A determination is made concerning the amount reasonably necessary to support the debtor and dependents and applied against any of the following: alimony or support; compensation for loss of future earnings of individual to whom debtor was a dependent; payments for life insurance insuring the life of an individual to whom debtor was a dependent; payments for wrongful death of person to whom debtor was a dependent; and payments under stock bonus, pension, profit sharing, annuity, or any other plan when payments are made based on the debtor's age, health, disability, death, or length of service.

All Other: There are 100 percent exemptions for the following: payments for disability insurance, health insurance, unemployment compensation, veteran's benefits, public assistance benefits, crime victim's reparation benefits, and social security benefits. Any professional prescribed health aid used by the debtor or a dependent is also totally exempt, as are most unmatured life insurance plans owned by the debtor, except credit life.

COLORADO

Wages: Seventy-five percent of all disposable income, or thirty times the federal minimum hourly wage per week, whichever is greater, including payments from pension, retirement, and deferred compensation plans, is exempt.

Motor Vehicle: There is a $1,000 exemption for a motor vehicle used either to get to work or in the performance of an occupation. This increases to $3,000 if the motor vehicle is owned by a disabled or elderly person and is used to obtain medical care for a disabled or elderly person.

Limited Exemptions: The limited exemptions apply as follows: household goods, $1,500; avails of life insurance policies, $5,000; provisions and fuel, $300; sickness and accident insurance benefits, $200 per month with no limit on lump-sum payments; personal library, school books, and family pictures, $750; library of professional person, $1,500; tools and equipment used in trade or business, $1,500; farmer's livestock and poultry, $3,000; farmer's machinery and tools, $2,000; jewelry and watches, $500; and wearing apparel, $750.

All Others: Unlimited exemptions are granted to the following: burial sites for family members; payments received for fire and police pension benefits, public employee and teacher retirement benefits, public assistance benefits, fraternal benefit society benefits, unemployment and worker's compensation benefits, crime victim reparation awards, proceeds of claim for personal injury, proceeds of certain life insurance policies, and armed forces pension benefits. Also granted a 100 percent exemption are professionally prescribed health aids and specific partnership property.

CONNECTICUT

Wages: Seventy-five percent of all disposable earnings, or forty times the federal minimum hourly wage per week, whichever is greater, is exempt.

Motor Vehicle: A maximum of $1,500 for one motor vehicle.

Limited Exemptions: The following are limited to the same exemptions as wages: payments for alimony and support other than child support; payments from profit-sharing, pension, annuity, or other retirement plans; and benefits paid under no-fault insurance claims.

All Others: Exemptions of 100 percent are granted for the following: family burial plot; books, tools, animals, and instruments required for trade or business; necessary household furniture, bedding, and appliances; necessary apparel and food; necessary health aids; items required of members of military or militia; residential utility deposits and one residential security deposit; liquor permits; and specific partnership property. Also 100 percent exempt are payments received as public employee retirement benefits, fraternal benefit society benefits, sickness or disability benefits, court-approved child support benefits, worker's compensation benefits, veteran's benefits, unemployment compensation benefits, and public assistance benefits. Also exempted are wedding and engagement rings and awards paid under crime victim's reparation act.

DELAWARE

Wages: Eighty-five percent of wages, salaries, and commissions is exempt.

Limited Exemptions: Persons residing in New Castle and Sussex counties may exempt up to $75 worth of tools and equipment necessary to conduct a trade or business. Those living in Kent County can exempt $50. A maximum income from annuities of $350 per month is also exempt. If the debtor is a head of household, a $500 exemption can be used to protect any personal property.

All Others: A 100 percent exemption is granted for the following: family Bible, school books, seat or pew in house of worship, family pictures, family library, burial plot, all wearing apparel, sewing machines, leased pianos and organs, and specific partnership property. Also exempt are payments received as Kent, Sussex, and state employee pension benefits; unemployment and worker's compensation benefits; fraternal benefit society benefits; proceeds of certain life insurance policies; public assistance benefits; and the proceeds of group and health insurance policies.

DISTRICT OF COLUMBIA

Wages: Seventy-five percent of disposable income, or thirty times the federal minimum hourly wage per week, whichever is greater, is exempt. This includes any compensation for personal services and periodic payments under pension or retirement plans. In the case of prisoner in a work release program, the wages are 100 percent exempt.

Motor Vehicle: A $500 exemption is granted for one motor vehicle only if it is used principally in the conduct of trade or

Your Exemptions

business. This exemption can be claimed for a cart, wagon, or dray and harness instead of a motor vehicle.

Limited Exemptions: The following amounts are the permitted exemptions for each item: family library, $400; household furniture and furnishings, $300; wearing apparel, $300 per person; tools and instruments of trade or business, $200; stock or materials necessary to conduct trade or business, $200; library, tools, and furniture of professional person or artist, $300; and mechanic's tools of person not principal supporter of family, $200. Up to $50 is exempt for shares and membership certificates in cooperative associations.

All Others: A 100 percent exemption is granted for family pictures; one horse or mule; food and fuel for three months; and the following payments: public assistance benefits, worker's compensation and unemployment compensation benefits, disability and group life insurance benefits, fraternal benefit society benefits, and teacher and public employee retirement benefits. Also exempt are specific partnership property and seals and documents of a notary public. There is a 100 percent exemption for proceeds from a wrongful death claim less amounts awarded for expenses of last illness and burial.

FLORIDA

Wages: The wages of the head of household are completely exempt. The head of household can include unmarried, divorced, legally separated, or widowed persons who provide more than 50 percent of the support for a child or other dependent. This exemption also applies to deposits in a bank account that are the result of wages.

Limited Exemptions: Up to a maximum of $1,000 can be exempted for any personal property.

All Others: A 100 percent exemption is granted for the following: worker's compensation benefits; unemployment compensation benefits; disability insurance benefits; fire, police, teacher, and public employee retirement benefits; disability insurance benefits; public assistance benefits; veteran's benefits; and fraternal benefit society benefits. Also exempt are the proceeds from certain life insurance, annuity, deferred compensation, and retirement and profit-sharing plans.

GEORGIA

Wages: Seventy-five percent of wages and payments from pension and retirement plans, or 30 times the federal minimum hourly wage per week, whichever is greater, is exempt.

Motor Vehicle: A maximum of $1,000 is exempt for all motor vehicles.

Limited Exemptions: There is a limit of $200 per item and a limit of $3,500 for the total of the following: household furnishings and goods, appliances, wearing apparel, books, musical instruments, animals, and crops held for family or personal use. The following limits also apply: tools, equipment, and books for professional or trade use, $500; personal jewelry, $500; total interest in dividends or interest or loan value of unmatured life insurance policies insuring the life of the debtor or someone to whom the debtor is a dependent, $2,000. Payments for personal injury claims are exempt up to a maximum of $7,500. A determination is made of what amount is required for the support of the debtor and the debtor's dependents in order to set exemption limits on alimony, support, or maintenance; payments under annuity, health, pension, or similar plans based on age, health, death, or length of service; payments for wrongful death claims on the life of an individual to whom the debtor was a depend-

Your Exemptions

ent, payment of a life insurance plan on that same person, or a claim for compensation of the loss of future earnings for that person.

All Others: The following are 100 percent exempt: worker's compensation benefits, unemployment compensation benefits, social security benefits, fraternal benefit society benefits, disability insurance benefits, certain unmatured life insurance plans, professionally prescribed health aids, crime victim's reparation awards, public assistance benefits, and public employee retirement benefits.

HAWAII

Wages: One hundred percent of wages, salaries, and commissions due for services during the last thirty-one days is exempt. After thirty-one days, 90 percent of the first $100 per month is exempt, then 80 percent of the second $100, then 75 percent of the monthly balance is exempt.

Motor Vehicle: An exemption of $1,000 is granted for one motor vehicle, based on the wholesale value.

Limited Exemptions: Jewelry, watches, and items of personal adornment receive a maximum of $1,000 in exemption.

All Others: A 100 percent exemption is granted on all necessary household furnishings, books, appliances, wearing apparel, as well as a burial site not exceeding 250 square feet. Total exemptions also cover tools, instruments, equipment, books, uniforms, and other items required for a trade or business. This may also include one commercial fishing boat and nets, one motor vehicle, and other personal property used for trade or business.

You *Can* Go Bankrupt *Without* Going Broke

IDAHO

Wages: Seventy-five percent of disposable income, or thirty times the federal minimum hourly wage per week, whichever is greater, is exempt.

Motor Vehicle: Up to $500 can be exempted for the value of one motor vehicle.

Limited Exemptions: There is a $500 per item exemption on each of the following, with a maximum of $4,000 for all combined: family heirlooms, wearing apparel, books, family portraits, musical instruments, household furnishings, and appliances, including one firearm, and any animals. A $1,000 exemption can be applied to crops growing or grown on up to 50 acres of owned or leased land, as well as 160 inches of water rights for irrigation of that land. Another $350 per month can be exempted from the proceeds of an annuity contract, as can $250 worth of personal jewelry and $1,000 worth of tools, professional books, and implements used for trade. Exemptions for the following are based on a determination of the amount reasonably necessary for the support of the debtor and all dependents: assets or benefits from stock bonus, pension, profit-sharing, or similar plans that provide payments based on age, length of service, disability, or health; benefits payable because of the death of debtor's spouse or someone on whom the debtor was a dependent; money received for alimony, support, or separate maintenance; results of claims for bodily injury of debtor or for bodily injury or wrongful death of person on whom debtor is or was a dependent; and all payments due because of disability or illness.

All Others: A 100 percent exemption is granted for the following: public assistance benefits; worker's compensation and unemployment compensation benefits; fraternal benefit

Your Exemptions

society benefits; public employee retirement benefits; disability insurance benefits; social security and veteran's benefits; financial responsibility deposits under motor vehicle laws; group life insurance benefits; assets and benefits of IRS qualified pension, retirement, and profit-sharing plans; arms, uniforms, and equipment of peace officer, National Guardsman, or member of the armed services; burial plot; necessary health aids; benefits payable for medical, surgical, or hospital care; and specific partnership property.

ILLINOIS

Wages: Exemption is 85 percent of gross earnings, or disposable earnings equal to forty times the federal minimum hourly wage per week, whichever is greater.

Motor Vehicle: Up to $1,200 can be exempted for one motor vehicle.

Limited Exemptions: A $750 exemption can be taken to cover tools, implements, and books required for a trade. A total of $7,500 of payments resulting from bodily injury to debtor or person to whom debtor is a dependent is exempt. There is also a general-purpose exemption of $2,000 that can be applied to personal property of the debtor. Exemptions for the following are based on a determination of the amount reasonably necessary for the support of the debtor and all dependents: wrongful death payments for the death of a person of whom the debtor was a dependent; alimony, support, or separate maintenance payments; and payments from a life insurance policy insuring the life of a person of whom the debtor was a dependent.

All Others: A 100 percent exemption is granted for the following: public assistance benefits; worker's compensation and unemployment compensation benefits; fraternal benefit society benefits; awards made under the crime victim's reparation law; property held in trust for debtor; social security and veteran's benefits; disability and illness benefits; wearing apparel; Bible; family pictures; school books; prescribed health aids; proceeds and cash value of life insurance policies and annuity contracts payable to spouse or dependent of debtor; interest in IRS qualified retirement, stock bonus, pension, profit-sharing, or similar plans; and specific partnership property.

INDIANA

Wages: Exemption is 75 percent of disposable earnings, or thirty times the federal minimum hourly wage per week, whichever is greater.

Limited Exemptions: There is a maximum of $4,000 that can be exempted for tangible personal property or real estate other than the debtor's place of residence and $100 for intangible personal property. Widow's allowance payments made on death of spouse are limited to $8,500.

All Others: A 100 percent exemption is granted for the following: prescribed health aids; public assistance payments to blind or disabled persons; group life insurance proceeds; wards made under the crime victim's reparation law; worker's compensation and unemployment compensation benefits; fraternal benefit society benefits; police, fire, teacher, and municipal utility employee pension benefits; proceeds of life insurance policies payable to spouse, children, dependent relatives, or creditor of debtor; proceeds of mutual life and accident insurance; arms, uniforms, and equipment of national guard member; and specific partnership property.

Your Exemptions

IOWA

Wages: Exemption is 75 percent of disposable income, or forty times the federal minimum hourly wage per week, whichever is greater.

Limited Exemptions: There is a total exemption of $5,000 on the following items: one motor vehicle, musical instruments, and the debtor's interest in accrued wages and state and federal tax refunds. Up to $10,000 can be exempted for tools, books, and implements of a nonfarmer. The same $10,000 exemption applies to the implements, livestock, feed, and equipment of a farmer. Household furnishings, appliances, and goods can be exempted to a maximum of $2,000. Wearing apparel is exempted to $1,000, plus the containers in which to store them. There is a $1,000 exemption for books, family Bible, portraits, pictures, and paintings. The proceeds and avails from accident, health, disability, or life insurance policies is exempt to a maximum of $15,000 if payable to the debtor's spouse or other dependent. If life insurance was purchased within two years prior to filing bankruptcy, and the proceeds are payable to the debtor's spouse or other dependent, the maximum exemption is $10,000. Exemptions for the following are based on a determination of the amount reasonably necessary for the support of the debtor and all dependents: payments from pension, annuity, or similar plan based on death, illness, or length of service and alimony, support, or maintenance payments. Finally, there is a $100 exemption that can be applied to any personal property, including cash.

All Others: A 100 percent exemption is granted for the following: 1 acre of land for burial plot; one shotgun and either one musket or one rifle; prescribed health aids; liquor licenses; wedding or engagement rings; specific partnership property; equipment required by members of National Guard and state guard; and payments received for public assistance, worker's compensation, unemployment compensation, federal pensions, assistance for adopted children, and public employee pensions.

KANSAS

Wages: Exemption is 75 percent of disposable earnings, or thirty times the federal minimum hourly wage per week, whichever is greater.

Motor Vehicle: A maximum of $20,000 is exempted for one motor vehicle. There is no limit in the exemption if the vehicle is used by a disabled person.

Limited Exemptions: Up to $1,000 is exempted for jewelry and personal ornaments. Another $7,500 in exemptions can be taken for household furnishings, tools, musical instruments, books, documents, livestock, seed grain, and equipment required to conduct a trade.

All Others: A 100 percent exemption is granted for the following: payments received for public assistance; worker's compensation; unemployment compensation; crime victim's reparation award; fraternal benefit society benefits; federal pension benefits paid within three months of filing and needed for support; and pension, annuity, disability, and death benefits of public employees. Also fully exempted are food, fuel, and supplies required for one year; a burial plot; a liquor license, club license, or malt beverage wholesale or distribution license; specific partnership property; and funds in a prearranged funeral plan.

Your Exemptions

KENTUCKY

Wages: Exemption is 75 percent of disposable income, or thirty times the federal minimum hourly wage per week, whichever is greater.

Motor Vehicle: A maximum of $2,500 is exempted for one motor vehicle.

Limited Exemptions: The following exemptions apply: $3,000 for household furnishings, personal clothing, and jewelry; $3,000 for tools, equipment, and livestock of a farmer; $300 for tools required for a trade; $1,000 for library, office equipment, and instruments of a minister, attorney, physician, surgeon, chiropractor, veterinarian, or dentist. There is a $7,500 exemption for payment of claims of bodily injury of debtor or person of whom debtor was a dependent. Exemptions for the following are based on a determination of the amount reasonably necessary for the support of the debtor and all dependents: alimony, support, or maintenance payments; payments for wrongful death of individual of whom debtor was a dependent; payment in compensation of lost future earnings of debtor or person of whom debtor was a dependent; and the benefits paid from pension, stock bonus, profit-sharing, annuity, or similar plans paid for reason of length of service, age, illness, or disability. Finally, there is a $1,000 exemption that can be applied to any personal property.

All Others: A 100 percent exemption is granted for the following: prescribed health aids: proceeds of certain life insurance policies; payments for fraternal benefit society benefits, health insurance plans, no-fault insurance benefits, worker's compensation and unemployment compensation benefits, public assistance benefits, public employee retirement benefits, and crime victim's reparation awards; and specific partnership property.

LOUISIANA

Wages: Exemption is 75 percent of disposable income, or thirty times the federal minimum hourly wage per week, whichever is greater.

Motor Vehicle: A 100 percent exemption is granted for one nonluxury automobile or one pickup truck of 3 tons or less and one utility trailer, if they are required for trade or used to travel to and from work.

Limited Exemptions: A $5,000 exemption is allowed for wedding or engagement rings.

All Others: A 100 percent exemption is granted for the following: most household furnishings and appliances; family portraits; military arms and accouterments (military decorations and medals); musical instruments; proceeds of most life insurance policies; most public employee retirement plan benefits; property of minor children; tools, instruments, and books required for trade; worker's compensation and unemployment compensation benefits; poultry, fowl, and one cow for family use; fraternal benefit society benefits; public assistance payments; gratuitous payments made by employers; required therapy equipment and health aids; crime victim's reparation awards; and one burial plot.

MAINE

Wages: Exemption is 75 percent of disposable income, or thirty times the federal minimum hourly wage, whichever is greater.

Motor Vehicle: One motor vehicle is exempt to a value of $1,200.

Limited Exemptions: The following limitations apply: $500 for

Your Exemptions

personal jewelry, excluding wedding and engagement rings; $200 per item for household furnishings, wearing apparel, appliances, books, musical instruments, animals, and crops; $1,000 for tools, books, and implements required for trade; $7,500 in payment for claim of bodily injury to debtor or person of whom debtor is a dependent, not including portions for pain and suffering; $450 per month in payments for individual annuity contract; $4,000 in accrued dividends, interest, or cash loan value of any unmatured life insurance policy owned by the debtor in which the insured is either the debtor or a person of whom the debtor is a dependent; and a miscellaneous $400 exemption that can be applied to any property. Exemptions for the following are based on a determination of the amount reasonably necessary for the support of the debtor and all dependents: payments as compensation for lost future earnings of, or for the wrongful death of, the debtor or a person of whom the debtor was a dependent; payments from stock bonus, profit-sharing, pension, annuity, or similar plans based on age, length of service, illness, or disability; and alimony, support, or separate maintenance. It is also possible to use up to $4,500 of the residence exemption for any other property.

All Others: A 100 percent exemption is granted for the following: payments for public assistance benefits, worker's and unemployment compensation benefits, state retirement system benefits, crime victim's reparation awards, veteran's benefits, disability and illness benefits, and social security benefits. Also receiving a 100 percent exemption are prescribed health aids; one commercial fishing boat not to exceed 5 tons; certain life insurance policies; six months' worth of food, seeds, fertilizer, feed, and other material needed for one growing season and all tools and equipment required for raising and harvesting food; one of every type of farm implement needed to raise and harvest agricultural products commercially; one cooking stove, all furnaces or heating stoves, and fuel not to exceed 10 cords of wood, 5 tons of coal, 1,000 gallons of oil, or its equivalent. Also exempted is the total value of wedding and engagement rings.

MARYLAND

Wages: The exemption in the counties of Kent, Caroline, Queen Anne's, and Worcester is 75 percent of disposable income or $145 per week, whichever is greater. In the rest of the state the exemption is 75 percent of disposable income, or thirty times the federal minimum hourly wage per week, whichever is greater.

Limited Exemptions: The exemptions for wearing apparel, books, tools, instruments, or appliances required for work is $2,500. Household furnishings, regular wearing apparel, books, pets, and other personal items are exempted to a total of $500. A maximum of $3,000 in cash is exempted, as is $2,500 or real or personal property that is selected by debtor.

All Others: There is no limit on the exemptions for the following: payments for unemployment compensation, worker's compensation, state employee pension benefits, teachers retirement benefits, fraternal benefit society benefits, and old age assistance benefits. Also exempted are burial plots; specific partnership property; assets and benefits of an IRS qualified retirement plan; proceeds of a life insurance policy payable to the dependents of the debtor; prescribed health aids; and payments for the death, sickness, or injury of any person.

Your Exemptions

MASSACHUSETTS

Wages: Exemption is 75 percent of weekly earnings.

Motor Vehicle: There is an exemption of up to $700 for one motor vehicle.

Limited Exemptions: There is a maximum of $3,000 for household furnishings excluding the beds and bedding; $200 for books and Bibles; $500 for tools and equipment of trade or business; another $500 for materials and stock for trade or business; $300 for food or cash to be used for food; $75 per month for fuel; $500 for boats, tackle, and nets if debtor is a fisherman; $200 for one sewing machine; $125 in bank deposits; $100 in shares in a cooperative association; $35 per week in liability insurance payments; $100 per week in pension payments; an amount necessary to pay rent, with a maximum of $200 per month; and up to $500 additional in trust company, bank, or credit union deposits.

All Others: A 100 percent exemption is granted for the following: wearing apparel; beds and bedding; heating unit; burial plot; church pew; two cows, twelve sheep, two swine, and 4 tons of hay; arms and equipment for member of militia; specific partnership property; and funds received as payment for public assistance, veteran's benefits, relocation costs; worker's compensation and unemployment compensation benefits, public employee retirement benefits, wages of a seaman, proceeds from a group annuity contract or group insurance policies, and funds deposited in payroll accounts.

MICHIGAN

Wages: Exemption is 60 percent of earned but unpaid wages for a debtor who is head of household and 40 percent for all others.

You *Can* Go Bankrupt *Without* Going Broke

Limited Exemptions: A $1,000 of exemption can be taken for household goods, furniture, appliances, books, and utensils. There is a maximum of $1,000 for items required for work, including tools, implements, stock, horses and harness, and one motor vehicle. A farmer is entitled to exempt 60 percent of the proceeds from the sale of milk and cream.

All Others: A 100 percent exemption is granted for the following: wearing apparel; family pictures; arms and equipment of militia member; family burial site; church pew; ten sheep, two cows, five swine, one hundred hens, five roosters, and six months of feed; proceeds of life insurance policy payable to spouse or children of debtor; six months' worth of food and fuel for the debtor's family; and specific partnership property. All the following payments are exempt: disability benefits, veteran's benefits, worker's compensation and unemployment benefits, fraternal benefit society benefits, public assistance benefits, and state and municipal employee retirement benefits. The exemptions include 100 percent of the deposits in an IRS qualified retirement, annuity, or pension plan, except those made within 120 days of the filing.

MINNESOTA

Wages: Exemption is 75 percent of disposable income, or forty times the federal minimum hourly wage per week, whichever is greater.

Motor Vehicle: One motor vehicle is exempted to a value of $2,000.

Limited Exemptions: Certain exemption amounts are adjusted biannually for cost-of-living changes. A maximum of $4,500 is allowed for household furniture, appliances, utensils, ra-

Your Exemptions

dios, televisions, phonographs, and food. A farmer can exempt up to $13,000 worth of farm machinery, livestock, produce, and growing crops, and office equipment used for running the farm business. Others are entitled to exempt a maximum of $5,000 for tools, equipment, office furniture, books, and other items used in trade or business. Life insurance proceeds if the beneficiary is the spouse or child of the debtor are exempted to a maximum of $20,000, with an additional $5,000 for each dependent. The dividends, interest, and loan value of unmatured life insurance policies are exempt to a total of $4,000 if the insured is the debtor or a person of whom the debtor is a dependent.

All Others: A 100 percent exemption is granted for the following: pension payments for public employees; payments from private retirement plans, including IRAs if needed for support; Bible; personal books; musical instruments; burial plot; earnings of a minor child; property of a business partnership; one church pew; wearing apparel; one watch; payments for veteran's benefits, crime victim's reparation awards, worker's compensation, unemployment compensation, personal injury recoveries, and proceeds of a wrongful death claim. Also exempted are payments from a profit-sharing, stock bonus, annuity, retirement account, or similar plan based on age, length of service, illness, disability, or death.

MISSISSIPPI

Wages: Exemption is 100 percent of earnings for the last thirty days, then 75 percent, or thirty times the federal minimum hourly wage per week, whichever is greater.

Limited Exemptions: A debtor may exempt up to $10,000 of tangible personal property of any kind, except wages, salaries, or commissions. Other limited exemptions are $50,000 in proceeds of life insurance policies payable to anyone other than debtor, $5,000 in proceeds of life insurance policies payable to debtor, and a maximum of $10,000 in proceeds for a personal injury judgment.

All Others: A 100 percent exemption is granted for the following payments for public assistance, worker's compensation, unemployment compensation, public employee retirement benefits, employee trust plan benefits, fraternal benefit society benefits, and disability insurance. Also exempt is specific partnership property.

MISSOURI

Wages: Exemption for head of household is 90 percent of disposable earnings, or thirty times the federal minimum hourly wage per week, whichever is greater. For all others it is 75 percent of disposable earnings, or thirty times the federal minimum hourly wage per week, whichever is greater.

Motor Vehicle: A maximum of $500 can be exempted for one motor vehicle.

Limited Exemptions: An exemption of $1,000 can be taken for appliances, wearing apparel, books, household furnishings, musical instruments, animals, and crops. Another $500 is allowed for jewelry; $2,000 for books, tools, and implements of trade; $400 for any type of personal property; and $500 per month in alimony, support, or separate maintenance payments. If debtor is the head of family, additional exemptions can be claimed on any property except 10 percent of any debt, or income, to $850 plus another $250 for each dependent child. Exemptions for the following are based on a determination of the amount reasonably necessary for the support of the debtor and all dependents: payments due to wrongful death of a person of whom debtor was a dependent and payments received from profit-sharing, stock bonus, pension, annuity, or similar plans where payments are based on age or length of service.

All Others: A 100 percent exemption is granted for the following: prescribed health aids; unmatured life insurance policies; payments for social security benefits, veteran's benefits, unemployment and worker's compensation benefits, public assistance benefits, disability and illness benefits, and most public employee retirement benefits. Also 100 percent exempted are burial plots up to 1 acre in size, funds deposited in a financial responsibility account with the state treasurer, and specific property of a partnership.

MONTANA

Wages: Exemption is 75 percent of disposable income, or thirty times the federal minimum hourly wage per week, whichever is greater.

Motor Vehicle: Up to $1,200 can be exempted for the value of one motor vehicle.

Limited Exemptions: A total of $4,500 can be exempted for the following, but there is a maximum of $400 per item: appliances, jewelry, household furnishings, wearing apparel, musical instruments, firearms, books, animals, feed, and crops. Up to $3,000 can be exempted for tools, professional books, and implements used for trade. Other limited exemptions include $4,000 for unmatured life insurance policies, $500 worth of shares in a cooperative association, and $350 per month in benefits from an annuity plan.

All Others: A 100 percent exemption is granted for the

following: payments received for social security benefits, veteran's benefits, unemployment and worker's compensation benefits, disability benefits, medical and hospital care benefits, maintenance and child support, group life insurance proceeds, fraternal benefit society benefits, public assistance benefits, and most public employee retirement benefits. Also exempted are prescribed health aids; burial plots; militia uniforms, firearms, and accouterments; and specific partnership property.

NEBRASKA

Wages: Exemption for head of household is 85 percent of disposable income, or thirty times the federal minimum hourly wage per week, whichever is greater. For all others the exemption is 75 percent of disposable income, or thirty times the federal minimum hourly wage per week, whichever is greater.

Limited Exemptions: Up to $1,500 can be exempted for household furniture and kitchen utensils; another $1,500 is exempted for tools and equipment required for trade, $2,000 of property belonging to a disabled veteran if the property was purchased or improved with pension money, six months' worth of fuel on hand, $5,000 worth of loan value on certain insurance policies, and 6 months' worth of provisions. Health and accident benefits are exempted up to $200 per month if made in periodic payments. If they are paid in one lump sum, the entire amount is exempt. There is also a $2,500 exemption for the personal property of a head of household who does not qualify for the homestead exemption discussed in the next chapter.

All Others: A 100 percent exemption is granted for the following payments: public assistance benefits, worker's and

Your Exemptions

unemployment compensation benefits, pensions of disabled veterans, annuity contract benefits, fraternal benefit society benefits, and most public employee retirement benefits. Also exempted is all necessary wearing apparel; all immediate personal possessions; burial lots; money deposited under the Motor Vehicle Safety Responsibility Act; property subject to a lien; interest in IRS qualified pension, profit-sharing, stock bonus, or similar retirement plans; and specific partnership property.

NEVADA

Wages: Exemption is 75 percent of disposable earnings, or thirty times the federal minimum hourly wage, whichever is greater.

Motor Vehicle: Up to $1,000 of the value of one motor vehicle is exempted.

Limited Exemptions: A maximum of $3,500 can be taken for the total of the following items: household furniture, appliances, wearing apparel, one radio, one television, china, linen, crockery, kitchenware, and personal effects of the debtor and all dependents. Other limited exemptions include $4,500 for a farm truck, tools, stock, equipment, seed, and supplies; or $4,500 worth of office equipment, professional library, tools, instruments, and supplies for trade; or $4,500 for cabin, dwelling, cars, appliances and equipment, and mining claim of a miner or prospector. There is a $1,500 exemption for books and an exemption for up to $350 per month in annuity contract proceeds.

All Others: A 100 percent exemption is granted for the following payments: public assistance benefits, worker's and unemployment compensation benefits, fraternal benefit society benefits, group life insurance proceeds, health and disability insurance proceeds, certain life insurance proceeds, and most public employee retirement benefits. Also exempted are mineral collections; art curiosities; paleontological remains; burial plots; prepaid funeral funds; property held in spendthrift trust (savings and loan); one firearm; all family pictures and keepsakes; arms, uniforms, and equipment required by law; and specific partnership property.

NEW HAMPSHIRE

Wages: Exemption for the head of household is fifty times the federal minimum hourly wage per week. Wages for minor children are 100 percent exempt as are the wages of a married woman against small loans where her husband is obligated. Debtors of small loans have a $50-per-week minimum exemption.

Motor Vehicle: One automobile is exempt up to a value of $1,000.

Limited Exemptions: These exemptions include $800 for school books, library, and family Bible; $1,200 for tools required for trade; $300 for domestic fowl; $500 for jewelry; $400 for provisions and fuel; and $2,000 for household furniture.

All Others: A 100 percent exemption is granted for the following: all necessary clothing; beds, bedsteads, and bedding; one cook stove and necessary related items; one sewing machine; a militiaman's arms, uniforms, and accouterments; one hog and pig and pork for same; six sheep and fleece from same; one cow; one yoke of oxen or a horse if used in farming or teaming; 4 tons of hay; one cemetery plot; one church pew; all pension and bounty money authorized by federal law; jury and witness fees; specific partnership property; and

Your Exemptions

payments received for public assistance benefits, worker's and unemployment compensation benefits, fraternal benefit society benefits, and fireman's relief and retirement benefits.

NEW JERSEY

Wages: Exemption is 90 percent of earnings if total earnings are less than $7,500 per year. For incomes over $7,500, the exemption is set by the court in each case.

Limited Exemptions: There is a $1,000 exemption for household goods and furniture; another $1,000 for goods, chattels, shares of stock, and personal property of any kind; and a $500-per-month limit on annuity contract proceeds.

All Others: A 100 percent exemption is granted for the following payments: public assistance benefits; unemployment and worker's compensation; military pay, allowances, and benefits of militia members; fraternal benefit society benefits; health and disability insurance proceeds; group life insurance proceeds; most public employee retirement benefits; crime victim's reparation awards; and civil defense injury and death benefits. Also exempt are wearing apparel for debtor and dependents and specific partnership property.

NEW MEXICO

Wages: Exemption is 75 percent of disposable income, or forty times the federal minimum hourly wage per week, whichever is greater.

Motor Vehicle: There is a $4,000 exemption for a motor vehicle.

Limited Exemptions: These exemptions are $1,500 for tools and equipment needed for trade, $500 for personal property of any kind for a married debtor or head of household, $2,500 for jewelry, $5,000 for benevolent association or society funds set apart for or paid to family member of deceased person; the minimum amount required for membership in a cooperative associations, and a special $2,000 exemption that can be applied to any real or personal property if a homestead exemption is not claimed.

All Others: A 100 percent exemption is granted for the following payments: worker's and unemployment compensation; proceeds of life insurance policies; fraternal benefit society benefits; life, accident, health, and annuity benefits, withdrawal or cash value to New Mexico citizens only; public assistance benefits; crime victim's reparation awards; public employee retirement benefits; and beneficiary's interest in spendthrift trusts. Also exempt are wearing apparel, books, prescribed health aids, specific partnership property, and materials, tools, and machinery used to dig, torpedo, drill, complete, operate, or repair an oil line, gas well, or oil well that are subject to a materialman's lien.

NEW YORK

Wages: Exemption is 90 percent of earned but unpaid wages received within sixty days of filing for bankruptcy.

Motor Vehicle: Up to $2,400 can be exempted for a motor vehicle.

Limited Exemptions: These exemptions are $600 for tools, professional books, equipment, and furniture necessary for trade; $400 per month on periodic disability insurance benefits payments, or full amount if paid in one lump sum; up to $5,000 in cash, U.S. savings bonds, tax refunds, or certain annuities, if homestead exemption is not taken; $50 for

Your Exemptions

family library; $450 for domestic animals and feed for sixty days; $35 for one watch; and $7,500 in payments for bodily injury claim on debtor or person of whom debtor is a dependent, excluding any amount paid for pain and suffering. Exemptions for the following are based on a determination of the amount reasonably necessary for the support of the debtor and all dependents: compensation for the loss of future earnings of the debtor or person of whom debtor is a dependent; payments received on account of wrongful death of person of whom debtor was a dependent; alimony, support, or separate maintenance; certain profit-sharing, stock bonus, and pension plans; and required health aids, including seeing and hearing dogs.

All Others: A 100 percent exemption is granted for the following: all wearing apparel; family Bible; school books; family pictures; one sewing machine; church pew; household furniture; tableware and crockery; cooking utensils; one stove and sixty days' worth of fuel; sixty days' worth of food for family; one refrigerator; one radio; one television; one wedding ring; military pay, pensions, medals, rewards, and arms and equipment of members of military; security deposits for rent, utility, and telephone service; proceeds of certain insurance policies; payments for social security benefits, unemployment and worker's compensation, veteran's benefits, public assistance benefits, and disability and illness benefits, and crime victim's reparation awards. Also exempt is a burial plot not exceeding ¼ acre and specific partnership property.

NORTH CAROLINA

Wages: Exemption is all wages received within sixty days before filing for bankruptcy, if need for support of debtor and dependents.

You *Can* Go Bankrupt *Without* Going Broke

Motor Vehicle: Up to $1,000 can be exempted for a motor vehicle.

Limited Exemptions: There is a $500 exemption for tools, implements, and professional books necessary for trade; a $2,500 exemption, plus $500 more for each dependent, not to exceed a total of $2,000 additional, for the total of all household furnishings, wearing apparel, appliances, musical instruments, crops, animals, and books; and another $2,500 for any property less any amount used for homestead or burial ground exemption.

All Others: A 100 percent exemption is granted for all prescribed health aids; compensation paid for most personal injury claims or death of a person of whom the debtor was a dependent; specific partnership property; and payments for social security benefits, public assistance benefits, unemployment and worker's compensation, fraternal benefit society benefits, group life insurance proceeds, crime victim's reparation awards, and most public employee retirement benefits.

NORTH DAKOTA

Wages: Exemption is 75 percent of disposable earnings, or forty times the federal minimum hourly wage per week, whichever is greater.

Motor Vehicle: Up to $1,200 in value may be exempted for one motor vehicle.

Limited Exemptions: There is a maximum of $200,000 allowable in total payments from all pension, profit-sharing, retirement, and annuity plans, and a maximum of $7,500 in payment of personal injury claims on the debtor or a person of whom the debtor was a dependent, excluding any amount for pain and suffering, or for the wrongful death of a person

Your Exemptions

of whom the debtor was a dependent. A head of household who does not claim the exemption on crops and grains (following) can claim either a $5,000 exemption on personal property of any kind or the following exemptions: $1,500 for musical instruments and books, $4,500 for livestock and farm implements, $1,000 for household and kitchen furniture, $1,000 for tools and implements of trade, and professional library and instruments. A single person not claiming the crop and grain exemption can claim instead up to $2,500 in personal property of any kind. All debtors can claim up to $100 for personal books. Any debtor not claiming the homestead exemption can claim $7,500 in any form, including cash.

All Others: A 100 percent exemption is granted for the following: all wearing apparel; family pictures and Bible; one year's supply of food and fuel; crops and grain grown on a maximum of 160 acres of land; church pew; house trailer or mobile home if occupied by the debtor; specific partnership property; and payments for social security benefits, veteran's benefits, worker's and unemployment compensation, Vietnam veteran's bonuses, crime victim's reparation awards, public assistance benefits, and all public employee retirement, pension, death, and annuity benefits.

OHIO

Wages: Exemption is 75 percent of disposable earnings earned in the previous thirty days, or thirty times the federal minimum hourly wage per week, whichever is greater.

Motor Vehicle: A maximum of $1,000 is exempt for one motor vehicle.

Limited Exemptions: There is a $200-per-item limit on the

following, and a total exemption for all of $1,500, unless the debtor does not take the homestead exemption, in which case the total of the following is $2,000: household furnishings, appliances, musical instruments, jewelry, books, animals, crops, hunting and fishing equipment, and firearms. Another $300 is exempted for each refrigerator and cooking unit, $400 for cash on hand or due, another $400 for any property the debtor selects, $600 per month in sickness and accident insurance benefits, and $5,000 in proceeds from a personal injury award to the debtor or a person of whom the debtor was a dependent. Exemptions for the following are based on a determination of the amount reasonably necessary for the support of the debtor and all dependents: compensation for loss of the future earning of the debtor or a person of whom the debtor was a dependent; payments for wrongful death of a person of whom the debtor was a dependent; and payments from certain private pension or annuity plans; alimony, maintenance, or child support; and assets and benefits of an IRA account or Keogh plan. Also exempt is $750 worth of tools, professional books, and implements of trade.

All Others: A 100 percent exemption is granted for the following specific partnership property; seal and register of a notary public; prescribed health aids; burial lots; and payments made for worker's and unemployment compensation benefits, crime victim's reparation awards, group life insurance proceeds, fraternal benefit society benefits, vocational rehabilitation benefits, public assistance benefits, and most public employee pension and retirement benefits.

OKLAHOMA

Wages: Exemption is 75 percent of all wages earned during the ninety days preceding the bankruptcy filing.

Your Exemptions

Motor Vehicle: A maximum of $3,000 is exempt for one motor vehicle.

Limited Exemptions: There is an exemption of up to $5,000 for implements used in husbandry on a farm or for tools and related items required for trade. In addition, a maximum of $4,000 is allowed for wearing apparel of debtor and family. The exemption on alimony, support, or separate maintenance payments is limited to the amount necessary for the support of the debtor and dependents. The final limited exemption is for $50,000 in claims paid for personal injuries, wrongful death, and worker's compensation benefits.

All Others: A 100 percent exemption is granted for the following payments: social security benefits, public assistance benefits, military pension benefits, the tax-exempt portions of IRS qualified personal or corporate retirement plans, unemployment compensation benefits, fraternal benefit society benefits, crime victim's reparation awards, group life insurance proceeds, and most public employee retirement benefits. Also exempt are war bond payroll savings accounts; one personal firearm; prescribed health aids; personal books, pictures, and portraits; burial plots; household and kitchen furniture; two bridles and two saddles; specific partnership property; and the following livestock and enough provisions and forage to feed them for one year: one hundred chickens, two horses, twenty sheep, ten hogs, and five milk cows and their calves under 6 months old.

OREGON

Wages: Exemption is 75 percent of disposable income, or forty times the federal minimum hourly wage, whichever is greater.

Motor Vehicle: Up to $1,200 is exempted for one motor vehicle.

Limited Exemptions: The exemption for household goods, furniture, a television, radios, and utensils is $1,450. Other limited exemptions include $900 for wearing apparel, jewelry, and other personal items; $300 for books, pictures, and musical instruments; $750 for tools, implements, horses, mules, harness, library, and other equipment required for trade, plus sixty days' supply of food for the animals; $5,000 in cash or bank deposits received for the sale of exempt property; sixty days' supply of food and fuel; $7,500 in payments for personal injury to debtor or person of whom debtor is a dependent, excluding any amount for pain and suffering; an amount reasonably necessary to support debtor and dependents from payments for alimony, child support, and separate maintenance. A maximum of $250 per month is exempt for annuity policy proceeds. There is also an additional $400 in exemption that can be used for any personal property except to increase existing limited exemptions.

All Others: Prescribed health aids are exempt, as are crime victim's reparation awards, pension benefits based on length of service, one rifle or shotgun belonging to someone over age 16, public assistance benefits, burial lots, civil defense and disaster relief benefits, fraternal benefit society benefits, worker's and unemployment compensation benefits, health and disability insurance benefits, benefits to injured trainees and inmates, state loans to veterans, proceeds of most life insurance policies, and specific partnership property.

PENNSYLVANIA

Wages: Exemption is all wages earned but not yet paid.

Your Exemptions

Limited Exemptions: The debtor can select up to $300 worth of any kind of property to be declared exempt. There is a limit of $100 per month on the proceeds or cash value of a life insurance or annuity paid to the insured.

All Others: A 100 percent exemption is granted for the following: wearing apparel; school books and Bible; sewing machine; property acquired after a court-approved assignment for benefit of creditors; uniforms, arms, and accouterments of National Guard member; tangible personal property at an international exhibition sponsored by the U.S. government; and specific partnership property. Also exempt are payments received for public assistance benefits, fraternal benefit society benefits, worker's and unemployment compensation, proceeds of group life insurance policies, proceeds of disability and accident insurance policies, veteran's benefits, most public employee retirement benefits, self-employed person's retirement fund benefits, crime victim's reparation awards, Financial Responsibility Act benefits, and the proceeds of certain other life insurance and private pension fund benefits.

RHODE ISLAND

Wages: The exemption for most debtors is $50. There is a 100 percent exemption on the wages of a seaman, an active duty member of the military, if the debtor was on welfare during the year preceding the filing, or if the wages are paid by a charitable organization to the poor. Also exempt are the wages of the debtor's spouse and minor children.

Limited Exemptions: Up to $1,000 of household furniture and food supplies is exempt, as is $500 worth of tools used in trade. Bibles and other books receive an exemption of $300, and there is a $50 exemption for membership in a consumer cooperative.

All Others: A 100 percent exemption is granted on the following: all wearing apparel needed by the debtor and family; one burial lot; the library of a professional person actually in practice; specific partnership property; and payments received for public assistance benefits, worker's compensation, unemployment compensation, fraternal benefit society benefits, disability insurance benefits, health and accident insurance benefits, qualified assets of individual retirement accounts, proceeds of IRS qualified profit-sharing, annuity, pension, or retirement plans, proceeds of certain life insurance policies, and most public employee retirement benefits.

SOUTH CAROLINA

Wages: There is no wage exemption.

Motor Vehicle: Up to $1,200 in value is exempt for one motor vehicle.

Limited Exemptions: There is a $2,500 exemption for household furnishings, appliances, clothing, musical instruments, books, animals, and crops; $500 for jewelry; $750 for tools, implements, books, and equipment required for trade. If no homestead exemption is taken, a burial lot exemption of up to $5,000 can be claimed. If neither a homestead nor a burial lot exemption is claimed, a $1,000 cash and liquid assets exemption is available. There is a $4,000 limit on the proceeds from a life insurance policy on the life of a person of whom the debtor was a dependent and a $25,000 limit on the proceeds of a life insurance policy payable to the debtor's spouse and/or children.

All Others: A 100 percent exemption is granted for prescribed health aids; specific partnership property; and payments for social security benefits, public assistance benefits, worker's compensation, unemployment compensation, fraternal benefit society benefits, veteran's benefits, alimony and support, illness and disability benefits, crime victim's reparation awards, earnings from personal services, proceeds from IRS qualified profit-sharing, pension, and other similar plans, recovery for personal injury or wrongful death claims for person of whom debtor was a dependent, and most public employee retirement funds.

SOUTH DAKOTA

Wages: There is a 100 percent exemption on all wages earned during the sixty days preceding the bankruptcy filing, provided the total amount is needed for family support. The wages of prisoners on a work release program are 100 percent exempt.

Limited Exemptions: A head of household is entitled to exempt up to $4,000 worth of personal property of any kind. Other debtors can exempt a maximum of $2,000 of any personal property. If a head of household decides not to take the $4,000 personal property exemption, then the following exemptions can be taken: $200 for books and musical instruments; $200 for household and kitchen furniture; $1,250 for one wagon, two plows, one harrow, other farm equipment, one sleigh, and tackle for a team of horses; $200 for a mechanic's tools and stock; $300 for a professional person's library and instruments; and 100 percent of the value of five swine, two cows, a team of oxen, horses, or mules, two cows, twenty-five sheep and their lambs under 6 months of age along with their wool and cloth, and one year's supply of feed. There is also a $200 exemption available to all debtor's for a family Bible and other books; a $250-per-month limit on annuity benefits payments; a $10,000 limit on the proceeds and cash value of a life insurance policy if the beneficiary is a spouse or child; and a $20,000 limit on health insurance proceeds.

All Others: A 100 percent exemption is granted for family pictures; a church pew; burial plots; clothing; one year's food supply; specific partnership property; and payments for public assistance benefits, fraternal benefit society benefits, most public employee retirement benefits, worker's compensation benefits, and unemployment compensation benefits.

TENNESSEE

Wages: Exemption is 75 percent of disposable income, or thirty times the federal minimum hourly wage per week, whichever is greater, plus an additional $2.50 per week for each dependent child under age 16.

Limited Exemptions: An exemption of $4,000 can be claimed for any personal property, including money in bank accounts. A maximum of $750 can be exempted for tools, implements, and books required for trade. The following limitations apply to the individual categories of exemptions, with the provision that all categories combined cannot exceed $15,000: crime victim's reparation awards, $5,000; payments for personal injury claims to debtor or person of whom debtor is a dependent, excluding money for pain and suffering, $7,500; payment for the wrongful death of debtor or a person of whom debtor was a dependent, $10,000.

All Others: A 100 percent exemption is granted for the following: prescribed health aids; specific partnership property; burial lot up to 1 acre; necessary wearing apparel and storage containers; family portraits and pictures; family Bible and school books; the assets of an IRS qualified retirement plan; and all payments for social security benefits, public

Your Exemptions

assistance benefits, worker's compensation, unemployment compensation, cooperative scholarship benefits, fraternal benefit society benefits, health and disability insurance benefits, and public employee pension benefits.

TEXAS

Wages: All earned but unpaid wages are exempt.

Motor Vehicle: See Limited Exemptions.

Limited Exemptions: There is a maximum of $30,000 in exemptions for all the items listed under this heading for a debtor who is head of household or a $15,000 exemption for a debtor who is single. This exemption includes household furnishings; necessary wearing apparel; two firearms; food in stock; family heirlooms; athletic and sporting equipment; implements required for farming or ranching; necessary tools; apparatus and books used in trade; and two horses, mules, or donkeys, along with necessary tack. Also exempt are any two of the following: a bicycle or motorcycle; a wagon, cart, or dray, along with required harness; an automobile or station wagon; a truck cab; a truck trailer; a camper truck; a truck; a pickup truck; plus all passenger cars and light trucks not used to produce income. Other exemptions include five cows and their calves, one breeding age bull, twenty sheep, twenty hogs, fifty chickens, twenty goats, thirty geese, thirty ducks, thirty guineas, and enough forage for them to eat; a dog, cat, and other household pets; and cash value on life insurance policy owned more than two years and beneficiary is a dependent.

All Others: A 100 percent exemption is granted for the following: specific partnership property and payments for social security benefits, worker's compensation, unemployment compensation, employee group life insurance benefits, health and accident insurance benefits, fraternal benefit society benefits, public assistance benefits, crime victim's compensation benefits, proceeds of IRS qualified pension or retirement plans, and most public employee retirement plans.

UTAH

Wages: Exemption is 75 percent of disposable income, or thirty times the federal minimum hourly wage, whichever is greater.

Motor Vehicle: There is a maximum exemption of $1,500 for a motor vehicle only if it is used in the debtor's work. This does not include travel to and from work.

Limited Exemptions: Tools, books, and implements required for the debtor's trade are exempt up to a value of $1,500. Other limited exemptions include $500 for personal heirloom or sentimental items; $500 for furnishings and appliances; $500 for books, musical instruments, and animals; and $1,500 for the cash surrender value on a life insurance policy. Exemptions for the following are based on a determination of the amount reasonably necessary for the support of the debtor and all dependents: assets and benefits of profit-sharing, pension, stock bonus, annuity, or similar plans paying benefits for reasons other than health or disability; proceeds of a life insurance policy payable to a spouse or dependent; and alimony or separate maintenance.

All Others: A 100 percent exemption is granted for the following: military property of a National Guard member; assets in an IRS qualified retirement plan, excluding contributions made within 180 days of filing bankruptcy; specific partnership property; works of art either produced by the

Your Exemptions

debtor or family members or depicting same; one clothes washer and dryer; one refrigerator; one freezer; one stove; one sewing machine; all carpeting in use; all wearing apparel; all beds and bedding; three months' supply of food and provisions; prescribed health aids; a burial plot; and water rights necessary to supply the homestead with water. Also exempt are the following payments: worker's compensation, Occupational Disease Act compensation; veteran's benefits, child support, health and disability benefits, unemployment compensation, public assistance benefits, fraternal benefit society benefits, and most public employee retirement benefits.

VERMONT

Wages: Exemption is 75 percent of disposable income, or thirty times the federal minimum hourly wage per week, whichever is greater.

Motor Vehicle: Up to $2,500 is exempt for a motor vehicle.

Limited Exemptions: Health insurance benefits are limited to $200 per month, but annuity benefits can be as high as $350 per month. Other limited exemptions are $2,500 for wearing apparel, household furnishings, appliances, musical instruments, books, and animals; $5,000 for tools and equipment needed for trade; $500 for jewelry other than a wedding ring; $5,000 for growing crops; $10,000 in a self-directed retirement account; $700 in cash in bank accounts; $500 in proceeds from a life insurance policy; and $400 in exemptions for any property. Exemptions for the following are based on a determination of the amount reasonably necessary for the support of the debtor and all dependents: crime victim's reparation awards; social security benefits; alimony and support; veteran's benefits; health and disability insurance benefits; payments from life insurance policy, annuity, profit-sharing, stock bonus, pension, or similar plans where payment is based on death, age, length of service, or disability; and compensation for personal injury, pain and suffering, wrongful death, or loss of future earnings.

All Others: A 100 percent exemption is granted for the following: prescribed health aids; refrigerator; stove; heating appliance; freezer; water heater; sewing machine; 10 cords of firewood or 5 tons of coal or 500 gallons of oil; 500 gallons of bottled gas; one wedding ring; most unmatured life insurance contracts; one cow, two goats, ten chickens, ten sheep, and one year's worth of food for all; three swarms of bees with hives and their honey; two team horses, steers, or oxen; two harnesses, two halters, two chains, one plow, and one ox yoke; personal earnings of a minor child or married woman; and specific partnership property. Also exempt are the following payments: juror fees, group life insurance proceeds, fraternal benefit society benefits, unemployment compensation, worker's compensation, fire insurance proceeds resulting from loss of exempt property, public assistance benefits, and Vermont Employees Retirement System benefits.

VIRGINIA

Wages: Exemption is 75 percent of disposable income, or thirty times the federal minimum hourly wage per week, whichever is greater.

Limited Exemptions: A veteran with a 40 percent disability can exempt up to $7,000 in any real or personal property. A householder can claim exemptions of $150 for a clothes dryer, $50 for provisions, $25 for fowl, $25 for hay or forage, and $1,500 for fisherman's or oysterman's boat and tackle. If

Your Exemptions

householder engages in agriculture, exemptions include $3,000 for tractor and $1,000 for fertilizer.

All Others: A householder, defined as anyone who maintains a household whether alone or with dependents, is entitled to a 100 percent exemption on the following; wedding and engagement rings; burial plot; wearing apparel; family pictures; books; beds, bedding, two dressers or dressing tables; carpets; rugs; stove; twelve dishes, knives, and forks, twenty-four spoons; one pot; six dishes, plus one for each person over 12 in family; cooking utensils; six pieces of wood or earthenware; one refrigerator; one freezer or ice box; one china cabinet; two basins; one dining table and six chairs; one buffet; one kitchen safe; one washing machine; one loom; one pair of cards; one axe; two hoes; 50 bushels of shelled corn or 25 bushels of rye or buckwheat; 5 bushels of wheat or one barrel of flour; 20 bushels of potatoes; 200 pounds of bacon or pork; one sewing machine; tools and utensils of mechanic; three hogs; one horse; one cow and calf; domestic pets; one horse team with required tack; one wagon or cart; two plows; one drag; one harvest cradle; one pitchfork; one rake; and two iron wedges. All debtors can claim unlimited exemptions for the following: rents and profits of exempt property; specific partnership property; growing crops; and arms, uniforms, and equipment of member of naval militia or National Guard. The following payments are also exempt: public assistance benefits; health and accident insurance benefits; most public employee retirement benefits; worker's compensation; unemployment compensation; burial society benefits; fraternal benefit society benefits; proceeds from group life insurance policies; and crime victim's compensation.

You *Can* Go Bankrupt *Without* Going Broke

WASHINGTON

Wages: Exemption is 75 percent of disposable income, or thirty times the federal minimum hourly wage per week, whichever is greater.

Motor Vehicle: One motor vehicle used for personal transportation is exempt up to a value of $1,200.

Limited Exemptions: Tools, instruments, and equipment for trade, $3,000; farm trucks, tools, stock, equipment, seed, and supplies, $3,000; library, office equipment, supplies, and furniture of a professional person, $3,000. There is a $750 limit on all jewelry, furs, and personal ornaments; a $1,500 limit on exemptions for household furniture, appliances, and home and garden equipment; $1,000 for books; and a maximum of $250 per month in annuity payments. Also exempted are a three months' supply of provisions and fuel and $500 of any other personal property the debtor selects, but not more than $100 of cash, bank accounts, and securities.

All Others: A 100 percent exemption is granted for the following: family pictures and keepsakes; all wearing apparel; arms, uniforms, and equipment of state militia members; family burying grounds; and specific partnership property. Also exempt are payments for fraternal benefit society benefits; public assistance benefits; most public employee retirement benefits; proceeds of group life insurance; proceeds from a trust benefiting debtor that was created and funded by another person; disability insurance benefits; unemployment compensation; federal pension benefits; industrial insurance benefits; fire insurance proceeds for loss of exempt property; and proceeds from IRS qualified retirement, disability, or death plans.

Your Exemptions

WEST VIRGINIA

Wages: Exemption is 80 percent of earned but unpaid wages.

Motor Vehicle: One motor vehicle is exempt to a value of $1,200.

Limited Exemptions: A debtor who is also a head of household can exempt $1,000 of personal property. All debtors can claim the following exemptions: $200 per item with a total of $1,000 for household furnishings, appliances, books, musical instruments, wearing apparel, animals, and crops; $500 for jewelry; $4,000 interest in certain life insurance policies; $750 worth of tools, professional books, and implements for trade; and $400 of any property the debtor selects. This can increase to as much as $7,900 if the homestead exemption is not taken full advantage of. There is a maximum exemption of $7,500 for payments received due to personal bodily injury of debtor or person of whom debtor was a dependent. Exemptions for the following are based on a determination of the amount reasonably necessary for the support of the debtor and all dependents: payments on account of wrongful death of a person of whom debtor was a dependent; payments for a life insurance policy on the life of a person of whom the debtor was a dependent; payments for stock bonus, profit-sharing, pension, annuity, or similar plan based on length of service, death, illness, or disability; payment for the wrongful death of a person of whom the debtor was a dependent; and alimony, support, or separate maintenance.

All Others: A 100 percent exemption is granted for the following: prescribed health aids; unmatured life insurance contracts; specific partnership property; and payments for social security benefits, unemployment compensation, veteran's benefits, public assistance benefits, disability insurance benefits, proceeds of a group life insurance policy, worker's compensation, fraternal benefit society benefits, and most public employee retirement benefits.

WISCONSIN

Wages: Exemption for debtor with dependents is $120 plus $20 for each dependent for a thirty-day period, not to exceed 75 percent of net income. A debtor without dependents can exempt not less than $75 and not more than $100 for each thirty-day period.

Motor Vehicle: There is a $1,000 exemption for one automobile.

Limited Exemptions: Jewelry and articles of adornment are exempted to $400, household furniture not listed under full exemption to $200, one firearm to $50, one tractor to $1,500, other farming tools and utensils to $300, tools and instruments for trade to $200, printing presses and material of a printer to $1,500, $200 worth of government bonds and savings stamps, and a maximum of $150 per month in accident insurance benefits. A debtor who does not claim the homestead exemption can exempt up to $1,000 in bank deposits.

All Others: A 100 percent exemption is granted for the following: one year's worth of provisions; wearing apparel; personal books; Bible; family pictures; school books; church pew or seat; one sewing machine; swords, plates, or other articles given to debtor by Congress or legislature; one television; one radio; all beds and bedding; all cooking utensils; eight cows; ten swine; two horses or mules; ten sheep with their wool; fifty chickens; harness; and feed for livestock for one year; one each of the following—wagon, cart, or dray, sleigh, plow, binder, drag, corn binder, mower, springtooth harrow, disc harrow, seeder, hay loader, and corn planter;

Your Exemptions

uniforms, arms, and equipment of National Guard member; books, plates, maps, and papers of abstractor; patents of inventor; cemetery lots and monuments; and specific partnership property. Also exempt are payments for social security benefits; worker's compensation; unemployment compensation; public assistance benefits; most public employee retirement benefits; federal disability insurance benefits; interest in employee and self-employed retirement, disability, death, stock bonus, profit-sharing, pension, and similar plans; veteran's benefits; fraternal benefit society benefits if premiums are paid by others or limit of $5,000; and proceeds of life insurance policy payable to another.

WYOMING

Wages: Exemption is 50 percent of all wages earned in the previous sixty days that are required for support of debtor and dependents.

Motor Vehicle: One motor vehicle is exempt up to a value of $2,000.

Limited Exemptions: There is an exemption of $2,000 per person living in the debtor's home for the following: household furniture, bedding, provisions, and any other household articles. The exemption for wearing apparel and wedding rings is $1,000. Up to $2,000 can be exempted for tools, stock, implements, library, and instruments required to conduct trade or profession. The proceeds from an annuity contract are limited to $350 per month.

All Others: A 100 percent exemption is granted on the following: liquor licenses and permits, earnings of prison inmates, the seal of a notary public, burial plot, family Bible, school books, pictures, and specific partnership property. Also exempt are the following payments: proceeds of group life and disability insurance, proceeds of life insurance if beneficiary is not the insured, public assistance benefits, unemployment compensation, worker's compensation, fraternal benefit society benefits, pension and annuity benefits of retired employees or self-employed persons, and most public employee retirement benefits.

Eleven

HOME AND REAL ESTATE EXEMPTIONS: A STATE-BY-STATE GUIDE

Because we are a constitutional republic, only a limited number of civil and criminal laws are dealt with at the federal level. Most civil and criminal laws are reserved for the states to legislate and regulate. As with most other matters, bankruptcy laws relating to exemptions are the responsibility of the states, with the exceptions of the limited federal exemptions. The widely varying exemptions demonstrated in this chapter represent the concerns and priorities of the individual states.

Most states exempt at least a portion of a debtor's home from being sold to satisfy debts. Because these homestead exemptions vary so widely from one state to another, it is not uncommon to find families facing the prospect of bankruptcy deciding to sell their home and buy a home in another state with the proceeds. They flee a state with either no homestead exemption or one with a limited homestead exemption in favor of a state with a substantially more generous homestead exemption law.

The discussion that follows is an explanation of the homestead exemption laws in those states having one. When

You *Can* Go Bankrupt *Without* Going Broke

you have reviewed these laws, you too may find it expedient to sell your home and move before you file a bankruptcy petition.

ALABAMA exempts a maximum of 160 acres and a home or mobile home to a total value of $5,000. A husband and wife filing a joint bankruptcy petition may double this value. The exemption declaration for the homestead must be filed with the probate court to be effective.

ALASKA exempts a maximum of $54,000 of the property used as the principal residence of the debtor or the debtor's dependents.

ARIZONA exempts a maximum of $100,000 of the debtor's equity in a home, apartment, or mobile home and the land on which it stands, provided it is used as the debtor's residence. The exemption must be recorded with the county recorder to be effective.

ARKANSAS offers two homestead exemptions from which a debtor may select one to claim. Option 1 permits a head of family to exempt property used as the debtor's residence to an unlimited value if it is located within a village, town, or city and does not exceed a ¼ acre in size or 80 acres if it is located elsewhere. If the property is located in a village, town, or city and is between ¼ and 1 acre, or between 80 and 160 acres elsewhere, the exemption is $2,500. Property size limits are 1 acre and 160 acres, respectively.

Option 2 permits a single debtor to exempt a maximum of $800 for property used as a residence or a married debtor to exempt a maximum of $1,250.

If the property of a deceased homesteader belongs to a widow or minor children, it is granted a 100 percent exemption, including all rents and profits earned, for the life of the widow or the minority status of the children.

Home and Real Estate Exemptions

CALIFORNIA offers several different exemptions for a homestead that includes a house, outbuilding and land, a mobile home, a boat, or condo or co-op apartment. A single person can exempt a maximum of $30,000. A family can exempt up to $45,000. A single person over 55 earning less than $15,000 annually, or a married person over 55 earning less than $20,000 annually, a disabled person, or anyone over 65 can claim an exemption up to $75,000.

COLORADO exempts a home or mobile home to a maximum of $20,000, or a house trailer or coach to a maximum of $3,500, provided it is occupied as the debtor's residence.

CONNECTICUT has no homestead exemption.

DELAWARE has no homestead exemption.

DISTRICT OF COLUMBIA will only exempt residential condominium escrow deposits of any size.

FLORIDA exempts the total value of a homestead up to 160 acres if it is located outside of a municipality, or ½ acre if it is located within a municipality.

GEORGIA exempts a maximum of $5,000 for a homestead, including a co-op if it is used as a residence.

HAWAII exempts a total of $20,000 for a homestead, unless the debtor is head of family or over 65, in which case the exemption is $30,000.

IDAHO exempts the house or mobile home in which the debtor resides and the land on which it stands to a maximum of $30,000.

ILLINOIS offers a homestead exemption that includes a farm, lot and buildings, condo, mobile home, or co-op to a maximum of $7,500.

You *Can* Go Bankrupt *Without* Going Broke

INDIANA exempts a maximum of $7,500 for a homestead.

IOWA offers an unlimited exemption for a homestead that is ½ acre or less if located within a city or town, or not more than 40 acres if located elsewhere.

KANSAS offers an unlimited exemption for a rural homestead of up to 160 acres. If the homestead is located within a town or city, it is exempt to a maximum of 1 acre.

KENTUCKY exempts a homestead to a maximum of $5,000.

LOUISIANA exempts a maximum of $15,000 for up to 160 acres of land.

MAINE offers a homestead exemption that includes a co-op or a burial ground to a value of $7,500. This may be doubled by joint debtors. If the debtor is 65 or older or is disabled, the exemption is $60,000.

MARYLAND has no homestead exemption.

MASSACHUSETTS offers a $100,000 homestead exemption, which may be doubled by joint debtors. If debtor is over 65 or disabled, the exemption is $150,000.

MICHIGAN exempts a maximum of $3,500 for a homestead that does not exceed one lot in a town, city, or village or 40 acres elsewhere.

MINNESOTA exempts a homestead without any limit, provided it is not more than 160 acres if outside a city or not more than ½ acre if within a city.

MISSISSIPPI offers a $30,000 exemption on a homestead of not more than 160 acres of land.

MISSOURI exempts a house and land for up to $8,000 and a mobile home used as the debtor's residence to $1,000.

Home and Real Estate Exemptions

MONTANA exempts a homestead consisting of a house or mobile home and the land it stands on for a maximum of $40,000.

NEBRASKA will exempt up to $10,000 for a homestead that does not exceed two lots if it is located within the city or village or 160 acres if located elsewhere.

NEVADA offers a $95,000 exemption for a house or mobile home and land on which it stands.

NEW HAMPSHIRE will exempt up to $5,000 for a homestead, including a manufactured house if the debtor owns the land it stands on.

NEW JERSEY has no homestead exemption.

NEW MEXICO offers a $20,000 homestead exemption, which may be doubled by joint debtors.

NEW YORK exempts a maximum of $10,000 for a homestead that includes land and dwellings, a condo, a mobile home, or shares in a co-op. This may be doubled by joint debtors.

NORTH CAROLINA offers a $7,500 exemption to a homestead, including a co-op.

NORTH DAKOTA exempts up to $80,000 for a home, mobile home, or house trailer where the debtor resides.

OHIO will exempt up to $5,000 for the homestead of a debtor.

OKLAHOMA offers an unlimited exemption on a homestead that does not exceed ¼ of an acre of land. If the property exceeds this, a $5,000 exemption may be claimed on up to 1 acre located in a city, town, or village or up to 160 acres of rural land.

OREGON offers an exemption for up to 160 acres of land outside a city or town, or one block within a city or town for

$15,000 if a single owner, or $20,000 if joint owners. A mobile home standing on land not owned by the debtor is exempt up to $13,000 if a single owner or $18,000 if joint owners.

PENNSYLVANIA has no homestead exemption.

RHODE ISLAND has no homestead exemption.

SOUTH CAROLINA will exempt a homestead, including a condo or co-op, to a maximum of $5,000. This can be doubled by joint owners.

SOUTH DAKOTA will exempt the full value of a homestead if it does not exceed 1 acre in a town or city, 160 acres in the country, or 40 acres of mineral land. Exemption includes a mobile home that was registered in the state at least six months before the bankruptcy petition was filed.

TENNESSEE offers a $5,000 homestead exemption for an individual debtor or $7,500 for joint owners filing bankruptcy together.

TEXAS offers an unlimited exemption for a homestead meeting the following size requirements: the land cannot exceed 1 acre if located within a city, town, or village or 100 acres if located elsewhere. A family can exempt up to 200 acres of land outside a city, town, or village. The homestead can be rented to someone else without losing the exemption, provided the debtor does not purchase another homestead.

UTAH exempts a homestead on a sliding scale. The basic exemption is $8,000, with an additional $2,000 added for a spouse and $500 for each dependent.

VERMONT offers a $30,000 homestead exemption that can include rents or other profits from the property.

VIRGINIA exempts up to $5,000 for a homestead, which may

Home and Real Estate Exemptions

be doubled by joint owners. A veteran with a 40 percent disability may increase the homestead exemption by an additional $2,000.

WASHINGTON offers a $30,000 homestead exemption, which may include a mobile home and the land it stands on.

WEST VIRGINIA will exempt up to $7,500 for a homestead, including a co-op.

WISCONSIN offers a homestead exemption of $40,000.

WYOMING offers a $10,000 homestead exemption that may be doubled by joint owners. The exemption for a house trailer is $6,000.

Twelve

WHY YOU SHOULD CONSIDER USING AN ATTORNEY

Do-it-yourself bankruptcy kits can be found advertised in classified sections of many publications. These kits usually consist of a set of forms, instructions for completing them, and general guidelines on what to expect once you file for bankruptcy.

In rare cases of personal bankruptcy, the debtor can complete and file the forms successfully. However, most often the advice and guidance of an experienced attorney is required. Rest assured, it will pay for itself several times over.

If you successfully negotiate with your creditors and are able to improve your financial situation dramatically, you will not need an attorney. However, if you have failed to convince your creditors to settle for a lower balance or smaller payments, or your creditors have referred your accounts to collection agencies, then now is the appropriate time to see an experienced bankruptcy attorney.

Even if you have not yet reached the point where collectors are harassing you, it might still be wise to seek the advice of an attorney who can help you find ways to resolve

Using an Attorney

your problems. Visiting an attorney who specializes in personal bankruptcy does not necessarily mean you will file a petition for bankruptcy. Part of the attorney's responsibility is to conduct a thorough review of your circumstances to be sure that bankruptcy is the best alternative for *you*. Once the decision is made, your attorney must then help you choose the appropriate chapter under which to file. These decisions require the experience and knowledge only a competent attorney can offer.

THE ATTORNEY'S ROLES

An attorney who specializes in personal bankruptcy actually has three roles if the client is to be well served. The first is that of an advisor, the second is as a negotiator, and the third is as your representative.

As Your Advisor

As your advisor your attorney must analyze your financial situation and counsel you on the best course of action. This could be a straight bankruptcy, a repayment plan, or negotiations with your creditors. Some attorneys will ask you to provide them with a list of your creditors and how much you owe them, along with other financial data, so they can be reviewed before your initial meeting. Others will tell you to bring everything with you to the first meeting, at which time it can be reviewed and discussed.

It is important that the information you give your attorney, either before or during your first and subsequent meetings, be complete and true. Under the emotional stress and embarrassment many debtors experience, they can forget or neglect to list all creditors, even those they plan to repay, or fail to tell the attorney about something they did which might not be permitted under the bankruptcy laws, such as a recent transfer of property. It is absolutely imperative that you be completely honest with your attorney. You will be wasting your money hiring someone to help you and represent you if that person doesn't know all the facts.

An important aspect of the attorney's role of advisor has little to do with the law. As we mentioned earlier, many people who are faced with the prospect of filing personal bankruptcy feel a deep sense of guilt at having gotten into the financial quagmire in which they find themselves. Shame over failing to recognize where they were headed, and doing nothing effective to prevent it, creates a feeling of isolation from people who are apparently paying their bills on a timely basis, and a fear of what "the stigma of bankruptcy" will do to them and their relationships with others.

A good bankruptcy attorney wants to help a client through the emotional as well as legal process of a bankruptcy. One way to dispel this guilt feeling is for the attorney to explain fully at the initial meeting between debtor and attorney that bankruptcy is a legal right under our Constitution and that nearly one million people now exercise that right every year.

As a client you should sense the empathy of your attorney, as well as the expertise the attorney brings to the resolution of your predicament. Because personal bankruptcy can be a highly charged emotional and psychological experience, it is important that your attorney be not only a legal advisor but a psychological counselor as well.

As Your Negotiator

Many bankruptcy attorneys are also trained and experienced negotiators. In fact, a bankruptcy specialist may spend as much time negotiating with creditors as in court, sometimes even more. Sharply honed negotiating skills may be just what is needed if your creditors fail to take your attempts at

Using an Attorney

negotiating seriously. Nothing will attract a creditor's attention more quickly than an attorney's letter.

Some creditors have lawyers on retainer or, if the size of their operation warrants it, have their own legal departments. These attorneys deal with debtors who try to negotiate a change in their payment schedules or balances regularly. Sometimes it is better to have your lawyer deal with the creditor's lawyer. Your position in the negotiations is then represented on a more equitable basis. When an attorney represents you, the creditor or the creditor's representative cannot exploit your ignorance of the law, and thus take unfair advantage of you.

As Your Representative

Publishers of do-it-yourself bankruptcy kits claim many bankruptcy cases are routine and that you can go through the process quickly and without a hitch. This is true—most personal bankruptcy cases are cleared through the bankruptcy courts smoothly. What the do-it-yourself salespeople fail to mention is that the reason so many personal bankruptcy cases move through the courts quickly and without difficulty is that these cases are handled by lawyers. We did not write this book to promote business for lawyers, but we would be remiss in our responsibility to you, our reader, if we did not reiterate the importance of having a professional represent you in the bankruptcy process. Representing yourself against the creditor's lawyers is tantamount to jumping into shark-infested waters. The stress and pressures you are already under because of your financial situation are more than enough. We recommend you not add to it by trying to handle the bankruptcy process yourself; seek competent help from an expert.

If any of your creditors challenge your filing in any way, your lawyer is there to protect your rights. A lawyer experienced in personal bankruptcy cases knows how to deal with your creditors' representatives and what they can and cannot do.

HOW TO FIND A PERSONAL BANKRUPTCY ATTORNEY

Personal bankruptcy is a specialized field of law. To be represented properly, you need a lawyer who has expertise in this field. To find an attorney who specializes in personal bankruptcy you can simply consult your local Yellow Pages under the heading attorneys or lawyers. Many telephone directories now include a guide that lists lawyers by specialty. However, this should be a last resort.

A good place to turn when seeking a bankruptcy attorney is to someone who has filed bankruptcy. You may already know someone. Perhaps a close friend or relative knows someone. Either way, ask that person if he or she wouldn't mind sharing some information with you concerning the attorney he or she used. Remember, since this is someone who has already filed bankruptcy, you need not be embarrassed to ask for advice or admit contemplating doing the same thing.

These are some questions you should ask someone who has already filed bankruptcy:

> How did they locate the attorney?
> Would they recommend that attorney to someone close to them?
> Was the attorney understanding of their problems?
> Was the attorney someone with whom it was easy to talk?
> Did the attorney fully explain the options other than bankruptcy, if they existed?

Using an Attorney

How accessible was the attorney to the client when his or her advice was needed?
What fees did the attorney charge?

Once these questions are answered to your satisfaction, contact the attorney and arrange for a meeting.

If you cannot locate anyone who has filed bankruptcy, which is unlikely considering the number who do so every year, talk with the lawyer you used when you purchased your home, or the one who handled your divorce, or the accountant who does your taxes. Most attorneys and accountants will be able to recommend a bankruptcy lawyer or at least put you in touch with a local legal group that can.

If you have no personal contacts who can help, you may turn to one of two legal associations which can provide you with lists of bankruptcy attorneys. One source is the local bar association whose members include attorneys in all fields. Most bar groups maintain a list of members, and their specialties, which is provided to the general public on request.

Another group to contact is the American Bankruptcy Institute. Although local chapters may be slightly more difficult to find than the bar association, ABI's member lawyers deal almost exclusively with bankruptcy cases. The ABI's national headquarters is in Washington, D.C. You can call the Institute at (202) 543-1234; a representative will direct you to a local chapter from which you can obtain a list of bankruptcy attorneys in your area.

How to Select the Right Attorney

Once you have a list, or even just a name of a local bankruptcy attorney, speak to the attorney directly. Keep in mind that this is someone whom you are considering hiring to represent you. If you cannot get past the secretary or legal assistant now, you may not be able to do so later. If the attorney is busy, leave your number and ask that he or she get back to you. Your direct personal contact with your lawyer is important from the beginning.

When you speak with the lawyer directly, ask a few questions to see if you get clear concise answers. Remember, if this person is going to explain to you what is happening during the bankruptcy process, you need to be sure you can understand what he or she is telling you. After having read this book, you should be much more knowledgeable about bankruptcy than the majority of people who call a lawyer's office. Demonstrate a little of that knowledge and see how the attorney responds to it. In all matters you must feel comfortable with the attorney you choose. This is someone in whom you will place a great deal of trust, so you do not want to engage a lawyer who is too busy to spend a few minutes with you on the telephone or who tries to intimidate you by speaking legalese.

Once you have selected a lawyer, ask for a one-hour consultation. Don't be put off if there is a charge for this. It is not unreasonable for lawyers to expect to be paid for their time. Ask if the consultation fee will be waived if you decide to retain him or her to represent you. Fees for this type of consultation vary widely from no fee to $500. Whatever the fee, it should be agreed beforehand that this charge will be absorbed into the total cost of handling your bankruptcy case.

When you first meet with an attorney, it is important to discuss every facet of your financial affairs openly and honestly. Probe the attorney for information that will help you decide whether he or she is going to try to push you into a course of action or if you will be advised of all your options and allowed to make your own decision with the attorney's guidance.

The single most important thing in selecting a bank-

Using an Attorney

ruptcy attorney is to have confidence in his or her abilities and to feel comfortable about speaking frankly. You should not engage an attorney who intimidates you or tries to make you act like a passive client who will simply follow instructions. Having read this book, you should be fully equipped and qualified to become an active participant in your own bankruptcy, which is as it should be.

Thirteen

HOW YOU CAN PROTECT YOUR ASSETS

Filing a petition for bankruptcy will not strip you of all your worldly possessions. As we learned in Chapters 10 and 11, there are usually many personal items that you can protect from seizure or sale once you have filed bankruptcy. A little preplanning on your part can help to protect as much of your property as the law will allow.

PLAN AHEAD FOR BEST RESULTS

There are three basic rules to follow when protecting your assets:

1. Plan well in advance of your filing.
2. Keep the "pig theory" in mind.
3. Stay within the applicable laws.

You have a better chance of protecting your assets and not running afoul of the law if you follow these rules. You must keep in mind that there may be some things that one

How You Can Protect Your Assets

bankruptcy court will permit that another court in a different part of the country will not allow. It will be advantageous to seek the advice of a bankruptcy attorney or other person familiar with the policies of the court in the jurisdiction in which you will be filing if you have valuable assets to protect.

The steps to protect your assets discussed in this chapter are applicable to most cases in most bankruptcy courts. There may be some minor differences in some jurisdictions, but the following steps are sure to offer you the protection you need. An extremely important point to remember at all times is rule 3—be honest and work within the scope of the law. If you blatantly violate or even stretch the rules concerning assets, you may endanger your entire bankruptcy filing.

Plan Well in Advance of Your Filing

There are no hard and fast guidelines concerning the sale or transfer of assets to protect them prior to a bankruptcy. The time to start taking steps to protect your property is the first time you sense the shadow of bankruptcy on the horizon. Too many people wait until they are ready to file and it is too late. A rule of thumb which will help reduce the risk of endangering your filing is to take whatever actions are appropriate to your situation at least 90 days before beginning the filing process.

Keep the "Pig Theory" in Mind

Taking steps to protect your assets before a bankruptcy filing tends to fall into a gray area in which the law is not absolutely clear. While in this gray area it may help to keep in mind a legal theory developed by Professor Barry L. Zaretsky of Brooklyn Law School. He calls it the "pig theory."

According to the "pig theory," the courts will accept questionable behavior when one is walking the fine line between what is acceptable and what is objectionable, until you become a pig about it. If you act in good faith and don't make a pig of yourself in attempting to protect your assets, you should be able to walk away from your bankruptcy discharge in better shape than someone who did not preplan.

Stay Within the Applicable Laws

Be well versed in which laws apply in your state so you know which assets need protection and which do not. Obviously, if your state exempts your home from seizure or sale during a bankruptcy, there is no need to protect it. On the other hand, if your state does not protect your home or only allows a minimum value to be protected, you may want to do what former baseball commissioner Bowie Kuhn and banker Marvin Warner did; sell your home and move to a state that offers better protection.

Selling your home and moving to another state may seem like an impractical step which is too drastic for a variety of reasons. Such a move may seem considerably more practical if you weigh the costs involved in a move against what you will lose, especially if your present state offers little or no protection for what is most likely your largest investment, your home.

The advice of someone familiar with the laws and the practices of the local bankruptcy court will help keep you from straying beyond the gray area into actions that the court will consider objectionable.

Your goal should be to arrange your affairs before filing bankruptcy so that the maximum amount of property can be claimed as exempt and the minimum turned over to the trustee for liquidation. There are two basic ways in which you can do this:

1. Convert your nonexempt property to exempt property.
2. Use nonexempt property to pay off debts that will not be discharged through bankruptcy.

How You Can Protect Your Assets

The law permits prebankruptcy planning, and even conversion of nonexempt property, because the goal of the Bankruptcy Code leans more heavily toward protecting debtors so they can get a fresh start and less toward helping creditors maximize the recovery of their debts. You have a better chance of your prebankruptcy conversion of nonexempt property being accepted by the court if it is viewed as intending to permit you to land on your feet after the discharge of your debts. If a creditor challenges your conversion and can show it was done to provide considerably more than a fresh start, it may be deemed objectionable by the court.

IMPORTANT STEPS YOU CAN TAKE

Keep in mind that taking action to protect your property from seizure before you file bankruptcy is a gray area and the demonstration of honest motives could go a long way in helping you protect your assets.

How to Convert Nonexempt Property Legally to Exempt Property
Cash on hand or in the bank, in excess of what your state allows you to declare exempt from seizure, should be converted from nonexempt to exempt property. Use that money to purchase clothing or household goods which are considered exempt in your state. You might also use it to purchase a life insurance policy or some other exempt plan.

If there is nonexempt equity in your home you might consider obtaining a second mortgage to purchase exempt assets.

Another area to review is property owned that might only be partially protected. For example, suppose you own a car which is valued at $3,000 and you plan on filing your bankruptcy petition in a state that has a motor vehicle exemption for only $1,200. You could sell the car for $3,000, purchase another car for $1,200 or less, and use the remaining $1,800 to purchase household furniture or other exempt property.

Many people overlook or fail to tell their attorney about funds they expect to receive soon, such as a tax refund or a small inheritance. If you file bankruptcy and soon after receive a refund check from the Internal Revenue Service or your state's income tax authority, that money may be claimed by the trustee for paying some of your debts, depending on your state exemption laws. If you expect to receive money from any source, it might be better to wait until the money arrives, use it to purchase exempt property or for current living expenses, and then file bankruptcy.

When converting cash or other nonexempt property to exempt property, be sure to verify that the exempt property which you are buying is not something that could be classified as "luxury goods and services." Property not required for the support of the debtor and the debtor's dependents falls into this category. The purchase of clothing or household items, even a major appliance such as a washing machine, could be presumed to be required property and therefore acceptable. One the other hand, if you sold your $3,000 automobile, purchased another for $1,200 to qualify it as exempt, and used the remaining $1,800 for the purchase of a diamond necklace which is exempt in your state, the presumption of the court might be that you sold nonexempt property (the car) to purchase exempt (the necklace) that is a luxury item not required for the support of yourself and your dependents. Such a presumption could lead to the necklace being declared nonexempt.

One way to overcome this presumption is to demonstrate that the conversion and purchase were made well before bankruptcy was contemplated. This could be demonstrated if the purchase was made before you met with an attorney who first suggested bankruptcy to you.

A danger of converting nonexempt property into exempt property is that the court might interpret the conversion or transfer to be fraudulent. Measuring rods used to identify such frauds are sometimes called "badges of fraud." Their existence acts like a red flag calling the attention of trustees and creditors to potential fraudulent acts. Such "badges of fraud" include:

1. Falsification of books and records
2. Transactions with relatives, especially between a husband and wife or father and son
3. Secret trusts which reserve benefits for the grantor
4. Transactions with persons known to be insolvent
5. Excessive security given (such as a $20,000 ring for a $2,000 loan) or the granting of unusual "bargains" by paying inadequate prices
6. Unfiled mortgages or security agreements

The Uniform Fraudulent Conveyance Act defines a fraudulent conveyance as a transfer that is made or an obligation incurred which results in a person being insolvent, or in which the person has not received a fair consideration. A fraudulent conveyance may also be a transfer made or obligation incurred with the intent of hindering, delaying, or defrauding creditors.

If you have engaged in an activity that might be considered a fraudulent conveyance, such as one of those identified as "badges of fraud," be sure your attorney is aware of it. If the transfers were made without actual intent to defraud your creditors, and this can be proved, the transfers at worst could be reversed. But, if there is a possibility of the court's interpretation leading to a serious question of fraudulent intent, it may be better to delay the filing of your bankruptcy petition for one year from the time of the transfer. In addition, in certain states some fraudulent conveyances may constitute criminal offenses.

How to Use Nonexempt Property to Pay Off Nondischargeable Debts

If any of your debts are unlikely to be discharged in bankruptcy, you may be able to sell property that is not exempt under your state's laws and use the proceeds to pay those debts. This is an important transaction because nondischarged debts will continue after the bankruptcy, and those creditors will have every legal recourse to their advantage, including garnishment of your income. When such debts exist, using property you are going to lose anyway to pay them makes a great deal of sense.

Once again you must operate within the framework of the law and do so as far in advance of your bankruptcy filing as possible so that your actions are not successfully challenged.

Besides paying nondischargeable debts, you may also wish to pay debts for which a relative or friend has co-signed or debts from a creditor with whom you want to maintain good relations.

When selling nonexempt property to pay off debts that amount to more than $600, be sure to wait at least 90 days before filing your petition for bankruptcy. This is especially important if you pay a past-due account which results in the creditor receiving more money from your payment than it might have received if the debt was still unpaid at the time you filed bankruptcy and your nonexempt assets were liquidated and the funds disbursed. Such an action may be considered a "preference," in which case the payment may be set aside and the creditor required to turn the money over to the trustee.

How You Can Protect Your Assets

If the creditor is an "insider" (such as a relative) with reason to believe you were insolvent when you paid the debt, you may have to wait a full year before filing bankruptcy in order to prevent the payment from being set aside and the money used by the trustee as part of your nonexempt assets.

WHAT YOU SHOULD NOT DO

Do not commit fraud of any kind. If discovered, you may have bankruptcy relief petition denied or held in abeyance. This means your creditors can resume action to collect, and even worse, you may have to face criminal charges.

Be honest about all your actions, including which steps, if any, were taken to protect your assets before you filed. The bankruptcy laws are written to prevent you from becoming destitute as a result of your bankruptcy, and the courts will tend to sanction many prefiling activities, unless it is clear you did them with intent to defraud.

Make sure that any buying, selling, or trading before your bankruptcy filing was done at the reasonable market value, not at inflated or deflated prices. When selling a nonexempt property followed by purchasing an exempt property, be sure you can account for all the funds. For example, if you sold your car for $3,000 and purchased one for $1,200 because your state's motor vehicle exemption is $1,200, you may be asked to account for the remaining $1,800. Try to spend that $1,800 on exempt property that is required for the support of yourself and your dependents, such as clothes, food, or household goods.

Be sure to wait the required time periods discussed earlier when you transfer nonexempt for exempt property. Do not make last-minute transactions the court will surely look on with disfavor.

Finally, study the exemptions for the state in which you plan to file bankruptcy. They are there to help you, so do not be afraid to take full advantage of them. If you wish to do something and are not sure if it is something a trustee or creditor might object to, get competent advice first. Always protect yourself from the temptations of fraud.

Before we leave this subject, a few words about credit cards are appropriate. After your bankruptcy, credit will be more difficult to obtain than it has been in the past. If your bankruptcy was not caused by irresponsible credit purchases to which you've become addicted, you will want to take some action to ensure you will be able to enjoy the conveniences that credit cards afford, such as renting a car, reserving hotel rooms or airline tickets by telephone, making purchases over the phone, and even writing checks at establishments which require credit cards as identification.

When your debts are discharged, the only creditors notified are those to whom you owed money. There is no broad announcement that spreads the word throughout the credit industry. With the number of personal bankruptcies approaching one million each year, such announcements would be almost impossible. So, if you have credit cards that do not normally permit extended balances, such as American Express, Diner's Club, or Carte Blanche, and they are free of balances, lock them away until your bankruptcy is complete.

If you have VISA or MasterCard accounts with no balances, put them away as well. If they have small balances, try to pay them off as early as possible before your bankruptcy filing. Do not use them until your debts have been discharged. The same is true of any other credit cards, including department store and gasoline company cards. When you file bankruptcy you are required to list all your creditors. This list does not have to include accounts that

How You Can Protect Your Assets

have no balance. Since you owe no money to their issuers, they are not considered creditors, and you will most likely not lose the use of the credit cards.

Because credit will be difficult to get after your bankruptcy, review your current credit accounts when you realize that bankruptcy is a real possibility. Try to pay off any accounts that have small balances. Once this is done, do not use them until after the bankruptcy. To do so would mean those accounts represent current creditors.

Life on the other side of bankruptcy can be so much easier if you can come through the process with some credit intact, especially credit cards which are so important in this plastic-driven society of ours.

Fourteen

YOUR LIFE AFTER BANKRUPTCY

Bankruptcy is not fatal. Life goes on after the court has granted you a discharge from your debts. The major differences are that there may be property you no longer own, you no longer have to pay the debts that were discharged, and credit will be a little harder to find. Getting new credit will not be impossible, simply more difficult.

The Supreme Court said bankruptcy offers "a fresh start." It is up to you how you use that fresh start. Depending on what caused your bankruptcy, you may want to develop and live by a reasonable budget. A visit to your local library or nearby bookstore will provide you with many fine books offering advice on establishing and maintaining a budget. If your bankruptcy was caused by something other than your spending habits, such as a business failure or medical catastrophe, then your spending habits may not require altering.

A record of your bankruptcy will remain as part of your credit history for ten years. After that it is supposed to be deleted. On the tenth anniversary of the discharge of your debts, you will want to check this out with every credit reporting agency you can locate. In the meantime, reestablishing good credit and obtaining new credit will, as we have already said, be difficult.

A recent study by the Credit Research Center of Purdue University produced some interesting and surprising results. After thoroughly analyzing the credit bureau files of approximately 10,000 people who had filed bankruptcy, the researchers found that it was considerably easier for these people to obtain new credit after their debts had been discharged than is commonly believed.

They found that those who filed were able to get new credit as soon as six months following the discharge of their former debts, and they were able to get loans about 65 percent as often as members of the general population. One reason for these results is that some creditors look on people who have filed bankruptcy, especially if they filed under Chapter 7, as good risks because they cannot file again for six years. According to Frank Szczebak, who heads up the Bankruptcy Division of the Administrative Office of the U.S. Courts, people who have had their debts discharged and "have any source of income at all are seen as good credit risks."

The Wall Street Journal reported recently that many consumer finance companies gladly lend money to discharged debtors because they already deal with high-risk borrowers and compensate for their losses through the higher than average interest rates they charge. The *Journal* also reported that many automobile dealers, hard pressed to unload huge inventories, are also increasingly willing to finance car loans for those who have previously filed bankruptcy.

According to a Sears, Roebuck and Company spokesman, the retail giant will continue giving credit to any of its customers who file bankruptcy, provided they agree to continue paying off their prepetition Sears charge account balances. You might be surprised how many other merchants will agree to reopen your account if you agree to pay off the balance that was discharged as part of your bankruptcy. If you can afford to do this, then it is certainly worth a visit to any creditor whose account you value.

REESTABLISHING YOUR CHARGE ACCOUNTS

There is no law against your paying off debts that were discharged. Paying certain debts does not obligate you to pay any others; it is purely voluntary on your part. But it can become expensive, depending on the balances of these accounts.

There are other ways in which you can get new credit which are less costly. Let's take a look at five of them:

1. Your existing accounts with no balances
2. Secured credit cards
3. Passbook loans
4. Debit cards
5. Secured loans

There are probably many other methods available that you can use to reestablish credit. We have selected these five because they are among the most commonly used by people who have filed bankruptcy.

Use the Charge Accounts You Saved

In the last chapter we told you to lock away those charge cards with no balances on them. As far as the issuers of those cards are concerned, your credit is as good now as it was long before you filed bankruptcy. If you were unfortunate enough to have high balances on your VISA and MasterCard accounts and were unable to pay them down to zero balances, you are still in luck if you put away your American Express and Diner's Club cards. You will most likely still be able to

Your Life After Bankruptcy

use these cards without any worry of being embarrassed while making a purchase by some store clerk telling you the account was closed.

These accounts can also lead to some surprising new credit. The following example is the true experience of someone who filed a Chapter 7 bankruptcy which included all credit card accounts, except for his American Express and Diner's Club accounts.

Mike Chamberlain's debts were discharged in 1986. Unable to pay down his VISA and MasterCard accounts, Mike was able to pay the small balances on a few department store accounts months before his filing. He had never taken advantage of the special privileges to extend payments on his American Express and Diner's Club accounts, so he never had a balance on them that he did not pay each month.

After his debts were discharged, Mike submitted applications for VISA and MasterCard accounts to several banks, but was always turned down because of his bankruptcy. One of the banks that turned him down was Citibank, which also owns Diner's Club. Two years after his bankruptcy, Mike received a letter from Citibank which said he was such a valued Diner's Club member that the bank wished to send him a preapproved VISA credit card. Mike was surprised because although he had the Diner's Club card for over a decade he had not used it often, preferring to use the American Express card. What caught Mike's attention was the word "preapproved." All the bank wanted him to do was sign the enclosed agreement and return it, which he did. To his surprise a few weeks later his brand-new VISA card arrived in the mail with a credit limit of $3,500.

You *Can* Go Bankrupt *Without* Going Broke

After about a year of using the Citibank VISA card, and making his payments well in advance of their due dates, Mike decided to apply for a Citibank MasterCard. On the application he listed his American Express account, his Diner's Club account, and his postbankruptcy Citibank VISA account. In less than two weeks he received a letter from Citibank which said it could not give him a MasterCard because of his bankruptcy.

Citibank's inconsistency in issuing a credit card to Mike—he got one when he didn't request it, but was refused when he did request one—demonstrates that even that giant bank has no clear policy for dealing with consumers who have filed bankruptcy.

Mike's experience is not isolated. Imagine how many other Diner's Club account holders received the same preapproved VISA accounts after their bankruptcy filings.

If you were able to lock away VISA and MasterCard credit cards with zero balances, you can now resume using them with caution. Do not do anything that might provoke the issuer to check your credit standing. What they don't know isn't going to hurt them.

How to Use Secured Credit Cards

A secured credit card is one which is issued by a bank after you deposit a prescribed amount in a savings account. The usual deposit is $500, but can be as low as $350. The bank then gives you a VISA or MasterCard with a spending limit equal to the amount of your deposit. The expectation is that you will maintain a good payment record with this secured account which will work in your favor when you apply for a regular unsecured credit card in the future. Some banks issuing these secured accounts will later offer to return your

Your Life After Bankruptcy

deposit and switch you over to a standard account, provided you have managed your account responsibly.

The bank pays a relatively low interest on your savings, usually between 5 and 7 percent, and charges generally higher interest on outstanding balances than regular VISA and MasterCard accounts, usually 18 to 21 percent. As with the standard VISA and MasterCard accounts, if you pay the full balance before the due date, there is no finance charge. When you use the card to make a purchase the salesperson or cashier you hand the credit card to has no idea it differs from any other card.

With as many as forty million Americans unable to obtain regular credit, the secured credit card industry is booming. Because of that it has attracted some unsavory characters who hope to get rich off the backs of consumers who cannot get regular credit cards. Most banks issuing secured credit cards, or the marketers who represent them, charge a "filing fee" or a "processing fee." Read the small print carefully before you hand over your money. This is especially true with the many secured credit card commercials currently appearing on television. Be especially cautious of ads with "900" telephone numbers. These calls are usually extremely expensive. In some shady operations, the telemarketers are trained to keep you on the line for a long time. Make sure the ad tells you how much the call will cost. If the charge is based on the length of time you are on the phone, and the cost of the call is not refunded if you are rejected, better look elsewhere.

Another offering makes vague promises about providing you with a credit card without revealing which bank issues the card. This may be someone who charges a high fee simply to send you credit card applications from banks with which they have no relationship. Of course, they cannot guarantee you will get a card.

You *Can* Go Bankrupt *Without* Going Broke

Still another deal to stay away from are the cards that look like VISA and MasterCard, but are only good for buying overpriced merchandise from the issuer's own catalog. These cards are practically worthless.

One final warning about secured credit cards. Check carefully who issues the card. Make sure it is a bank where deposits are insured with the Federal Deposit Insurance Corporation. If the issuer is not a member of the FDIC, your deposit may not be insured, and you are best advised to look elsewhere. One company that issued both VISA and MasterCard credit cards without the backing of a bank was MoneyCard Systems. When the company went under, the deposits of those who held secured credit cards went with it.

There are many legitimate banks issuing secured VISA and MasterCard accounts and the number grows daily. In fact, competition among them has generated an open market, so before you sign with any bank do some shopping. Check the interest rates involved, the fees charged for annual membership, late fees, charges for exceeding your credit limit, and so on, and compare them to other banks with secured credit cards.

Two organizations sell lists of banks offering secured credit cards and details on how they operate. You may want to write to both of them before you apply for a secured credit card.

> For a list of 20 banks, send $5.00 to
> RAM Research
> Box 1700 (College Estates)
> Frederick, MD 21701

> For a list of 16 banks, send $3.00 to
> Bankcard Holders of America
> 560 Herndon Parkway, Suite 120
> Herndon, VA 22070

Your Life After Bankruptcy

USE BANK ACCOUNTS FOR CREDIT

Even if you have a small balance you are able to keep in a savings or a checking account, that small sum could make new credit possible for you.

Take Out a Passbook Loan

Passbook loans were common years ago, before the advent of universal credit cards and instant credit. It is basically a simple process. Deposit your money into a regular passbook savings account at your bank, and you will receive approval to borrow against your balance. Some banks limit the amount you can borrow, while others will approve a loan for the total balance of your savings account. Your savings account pays the bank's regular interest rate for this type of account, while the interest charged on the loan is usually less than the bank charges for unsecured loans.

Since this is an exercise designed to improve your credit standing, be sure the bank reports the loan and your excellent repayment record to the credit bureau it uses so it is incorporated into your credit history. Not all banks report these loans; be sure yours does, or your purpose will be defeated.

Debit Cards Will Help You

Debit cards are a cross between a credit card and writing a check. These cards look almost identical to a credit card. The major difference between debit cards and credit cards is that the funds to pay for a purchase made with a debit card are taken directly from your savings or checking account. Banks issue debit cards with limits based on the amount of money you deposit in a specified account.

Using a debit card may help you establish a relationship with a bank that might consider giving you a regular credit card at a later date. Since debit cards look like real credit cards, they are especially useful to people who cannot get "the real thing." Carrying a debit card can spare you the embarrassment of explaining to store clerks that you don't have a credit card which can be used for identification when you want to make a purchase with a check or you wish to order something over the telephone.

Apply for a Secured Loan

It may seem impossible to find someone who will extend you credit after bankruptcy, but one place to look where success is not so elusive is the purchase of an item that can be easily repossessed. Although no one in business wants to resort to retrieving used merchandise, in some industries, in certain situations, many retailers will take the risk. A good prospect for this is the automobile dealer who is overstocked. Beginning in early 1991, and perhaps even earlier, many auto dealers recognized that the millions of people who recently filed bankruptcy are an important market. As a result, an increasing number of dealerships advertise that they will extend credit to many people who otherwise would not qualify, including those with a bankruptcy in their background.

Another source of credit is a local retailer, especially a small department store or small chain. A personal meeting with the store's owner or manager, explaining honestly your bankruptcy and your present circumstance may get you a card with a small limit. That is not a bad place to start.

PROTECT YOUR NEW CREDIT

Keep Your Credit Files Clean

During the period of rebuilding your credit, keep track of the information various credit reporting agencies have in your file. Use the methods discussed in Chapter 2 to review this information periodically. Make sure obsolete and inaccurate data are removed or corrected. Keep in mind that no matter how hard you work to rebuild your credit, outdated or incorrect negative information in your file will hurt you.

A Final Warning

Because so many millions of Americans are unable to obtain credit for a variety of reasons, they have become the target of unscrupulous operators offering everything from high-priced information on secured credit cards to promises of cleaning up your credit history. Stay away from both groups. As we said earlier, lists of insured banks offering legitimate secured credit cards are reasonable in cost and easy to obtain.

The second group, usually called "credit repair clinics," can be downright dangerous, as well as costly. You have probably seen their advertisements in newspapers and magazines, with bold headlines promising to erase negative information in your credit files. Don't believe them. If the negative information in your file is obsolete or incorrect, you can get it deleted yourself with little or no cost by using the methods discussed in Chapter 2 of this book. There is no need to pay these people hundreds or even thousands of dollars to do it for you. If the information is correct, no amount of effort on anyone's part will force the credit reporting agencies to delete it.

Credit repair clinics are such shady operations that many states strictly regulate their activities, while some prohibit them from doing business at all.

A GLOSSARY OF TERMS YOU SHOULD KNOW

Acceleration clause   A provision contained in some credit agreements which permits the creditor to demand payment in full if the debtor defaults.

Arrears   A term used to describe a debt or loan that is not paid on the date the payment is due.

Attachment   The process of seizing a debtor's property once a judgment has been taken against the debtor.

Bankruptcy   The condition that exists when a debtor is no longer able to pay debts and uses the protection of the law to either liquidate property or reorganize affairs.

Bankruptcy Code   The federal law that governs all bankruptcy proceedings throughout the country.

Bankruptcy court   Special federal courts created exclusively to handle bankruptcy cases.

Bankruptcy estate   The property of a debtor who has filed bankruptcy, which comes under the jurisdiction of the court and trustee.

Glossary of Terms

Bankruptcy trustee   The person selected by the court to take control of the debtor's estate and handle any actions on behalf of the estate.

Collateral   Property of any kind that is pledged to a creditor if a debt or loan is not repaid on time.

Co-signer   Someone who signs a credit or loan application in addition to the person seeking the loan. By doing so the co-signer agrees to repay the loan if the signer fails to repay it.

Creditor   A person or business that is owed money.

Credit file   Credit and other information maintained by a credit reporting agency on almost everyone in the country. It is based on information supplied primarily by creditors. Since the information is not verified before it is placed in your file, there is a great potential for error. The credit reporting agencies supply this information to creditors, employers, and others.

Credit rating   A point system used by many lenders and credit companies to help determine if they will lend money or extend credit. It is calculated based on the information in your credit file.

Debtor   A person or business that owes a debt.

Default judgment   A judgment awarded to the party who files a lawsuit and the person being sued fails to respond within the time proscribed by the law. The filing party is then considered the winner of the suit.

Delinquent   A credit or loan account which is past due.

Discharge   The cancellation of an obligation.

Discharged debts   Debts that are no longer legally obligated to be paid as a result of a bankruptcy.

Glossary of Terms

Disposable earnings The amount of earnings left to spend after deductions required by law, such as taxes and usual living expenses, have been taken into account.

Equity The value of property in excess of the amount owed on any existing mortgages.

Execution The process of enforcing a judgment.

Exempt property Property that cannot be taken if a petition for bankruptcy is filed.

Foreclosure The process by which a mortgage holder can take possession of the mortgaged property because of default.

Garnishment The legal process by which a debtor's property, money, or credits under another person's control are applied as payment of a debt.

Judgment The determination of law as the result of an action in court as to whether a legal duty or liability exists.

Nonexempt property Property that can be taken and sold in order to repay debts.

Personal property Items not classified as real property, such as jewelry, furniture, and automobiles.

Real property Land and the structures permanently attached to the land.

Repossession An action taken by a lender or creditor to take possession of something you have pledged as collateral or used the credit to purchase, if you fail to make the required payments.

Secured credit Credit that is granted based on the amount of money deposited with the creditor. Examples are secured credit cards and passbook loans. It is also credit extended

Glossary of Terms

based on the use of real or personal property used as collateral.

Secured creditor A person or company that grants credit or approves a loan based on a pledge of real or personal property as collateral.

Secured debt A debt that is based on the use of property as collateral.

Unsecured creditor A creditor who grants credit or a loan based solely on a promise to repay it.

Unsecured debt Money owed for which property was not used as collateral.

Wage attachment Legal action taken by a debtor which forces an employer to deduct a specified amount of money from someone's pay before it is paid and send that money to the creditor until the debt is repaid. This is sometimes referred to as a "garnishee."

Appendix A

FEDERAL BANKRUPTCY EXEMPTIONS

Because personal bankruptcy is a federal issue conducted in federal courts, the federal government established a set of exemptions intended to aid individuals who have filed a petition for bankruptcy gain the "fresh start" the Supreme Court discussed. The majority of states have decreed their own bankruptcy exemptions which supersede the federal exemptions. Thirteen states and the District of Columbia permit a person filing bankruptcy to choose between the state or federal exemptions. If the state in which you plan to file bankruptcy is among these, you must compare the federal and state exemption options carefully so you can select the one best suited to your situation.

In addition to the District of Columbia, the following states permit the use of the federal bankruptcy exemptions: Connecticut, Hawaii, Massachusetts, Michigan, Minnesota, New Jersey, New Mexico, Pennsylvania, Rhode Island, Texas, Vermont, Washington, and Wisconsin.

The following is a description of the federal exemptions.

Federal Bankruptcy Exemptions

Real Property: The debtor's interest in a home used as a residence, or interest in a cooperative that owns the property used as a residence, or the burial plot for a debtor or dependents is exempt to a total of $7,500.

Wages: There is no federal exemption for wages.

Motor Vehicle: A motor vehicle is exempt to a total value of $1,200.

Limited Exemptions: A total of $4,000 may be exempted on the following, with a limit of $200 per item: household furnishings, household goods, appliances, books, clothing, musical instruments, animals, and crops. Personal jewelry is exempted to a value of $500. Up to $7,500 in exemptions can be taken for tools, books, and implements required for the debtor's trade or business. Another $7,500 can be taken for payments received on account of personal bodily injury to the debtor or a person of whom the debtor is a dependent. The value of unmatured life insurance policies in which the insured is the debtor or a person of whom the debtor is a dependent is exempt to $4,000. The debtor can exempt any other personal property up to a value of $3,750 by combining a "wild card" exemption of $400 with any unused portion of the real property exemption. Exemptions for the following are based on a determination of the amount reasonably necessary for the support of the debtor and all dependents: alimony, support, separate maintenance, and payments from stock bonus, profit-sharing, annuity, or similar plans based on age, death, length of service, or illness.

All Others: A 100 percent exemption is granted for the following payments in compensation for the loss of future earnings of the debtor or a person of whom the debtor is a dependent; payments for the wrongful death of any person of

Federal Bankruptcy Exemptions

whom the debtor was a dependent; crime victim's reparation law benefits; and benefits for veteran, disability, illness, unemployment, social security, and public assistance. Also exempt are prescribed health aids.

Appendix B

SAMPLE BANKRUPTCY FORMS

On the following pages are completed examples of the petitions, schedules, statements of affairs, and related items used in the filing of a Chapter 7 bankruptcy case. These have been included solely to illustrate what forms are involved in this type of bankruptcy filing, and how they are completed for a particular case. These examples are intended as a guide to help you become familiar with the forms and should not be relied on by anyone attempting to file a bankruptcy case without professional guidance.

Sample Bankruptcy Forms

Form 1, P1 (6-90)   Julius Blumberg, Inc. NYC 10013

FORM 1 VOLUNTARY PETITION

United States Bankruptcy Court	VOLUNTARY PETITION
CENTRAL District of ANY STATE	
IN RE (Name of debtor-If individual, enter Last, First, Middle) Debtor/Robert Paul	NAME OF JOINT DEBTOR (Spouse) (Last, First, Middle) Debtor/Jane
ALL OTHER NAMES used by debtor in the last 6 years (Include married, maiden and trade names) Debtor/Robert P.	ALL OTHER NAMES used by the joint debtor in the last 6 years (Include married, maiden and trade names.) Reardon/Jane (Maiden name)
SOC. SEC./TAX I.D. NO. (If more than one, state all) 123-45-6789	SOC. SEC./TAX I.D. NO.(If more than one, state all) 987-65-4321
STREET ADDRESS OF DEBTOR (No. and street, city, state, zip) 101 East First Street - Apt. No. 6A Any City, Any State 82437	STREET ADDRESS OF JOINT DEBTOR (No. and street, city, state, zip) 101 East First Street - Apt. No. 6A Any City, Any State 82437
COUNTY OF RESIDENCE OR PRINCIPAL PLACE OF BUSINESS Any County	COUNTY OF RESIDENCE OR PRINCIPAL PLACE OF BUSINESS Any County
MAILING ADDRESS OF DEBTOR (If different from street address) P.O. Box 681 Any City, Any State 82430	MAILING ADDRESS OF JOINT DEBTOR (If different from street address) P.O. Box 681 Any City, Any State 82430
LOCATION OF PRINCIPAL ASSETS OF BUSINESS DEBTOR (If different from addresses listed above)	☒ Debtor has been domiciled or has had a residence, principal place of business or principal assets in this District for 180 days immediately preceding the date of this petition or for a longer part of such 180 days than in any other District. ☐ There is a bankruptcy case concerning debtor's affiliate, general partner or partnership pending in this District.

INFORMATION REGARDING DEBTOR (Check applicable boxes)

TYPE OF DEBTOR	CHAPTER OR SECTION OF BANKRUPTCY CODE UNDER WHICH THE PETITION IS FILED (Check one box)
☒ Individual ☐ Corporation Publicly Held ☐ Joint (H&W) ☐ Corporation Not Publicly Held ☐ Partnership ☐ Municipality ☐ Other _____	☒ Chapter 7 ☐ Chapter 11 ☐ Chapter 13 ☐ Chapter 9 ☐ Chapter 12 ☐ § 304-Case Ancillary to Foreign Proceeding FILING FEE (Check one box) ☒ Filing fee attached. ☐ Filing fee to be paid in installments. (Applicable to individuals only) Must attach signed application for the court's consideration certifying that the debtor is unable to pay fee except in installments. Rule 1006(b). see Official Form No..3
NATURE OF DEBT ☒ Non-Business Consumer ☐ Business - Complete A&B below A. TYPE OF BUSINESS (check one box) ☐ Farming ☐ Transportation ☐ Commodity Broker ☐ Professional ☐ Manufacturing/Mining ☐ Construction ☐ Retail/Wholesale ☐ Real Estate ☐ Railroad ☐ Stockbroker ☐ Other Business B. BRIEFLY DESCRIBE NATURE OF BUSINESS	NAME AND ADDRESS OF LAW FIRM OR ATTORNEY Allen B. Attorney 541 East Eighth Street Any City, Any State 83872 Telephone No. (909) 846-5283 NAME(S) OF ATTORNEY(S) DESIGNATED TO REPRESENT THE DEBTOR ☐ Debtor is not represented by an attorney
STATISTICAL ADMINISTRATIVE INFORMATION (28 U.S.C. § 604) (Estimates only) (Check applicable boxes)	THIS SPACE FOR COURT USE ONLY

☒ Debtor estimates that funds will be available for distribution to unsecured creditors.
☐ Debtor estimates that after any exempt property is excluded and administrative expenses paid, there will be no funds available for distribution to unsecured creditors.

ESTIMATED NUMBER OF CREDITORS
☒ 1-15 ☐ 16-49 ☐ 50-99 ☐ 100-199 ☐ 200-999 ☐ 1000-over

ESTIMATED ASSETS (in thousands of dollars)
☒ Under 50 ☐ 50-99 ☐ 100-499 ☐ 500-999 ☐ 1000-9999 ☐ 10,000-99,000 ☐ over 100,000

ESTIMATED LIABILITIES (in thousands of dollars)
☒ Under 50 ☐ 50-99 ☐ 100-499 ☐ 500-999 ☐ 1000-9999 ☐ 10,000-99,000 ☐ over 100,000

ESTIMATED NUMBER OF EMPLOYEES -CH 11 & 12 ONLY
☐ 0 ☐ 1-19 ☐ 20-99 ☐ 100-999 ☐ 1000-over

ESTIMATED NO. OF EQUITY SECURITY HOLDERS - CH 11 & 12 ONLY
☐ 0 ☐ 1-19 ☐ 20-99 ☐ 100-499 ☐ 500-over

Forms may be purchased from Julius Blumberg, Inc., NYC 10013, or any of its dealers. Reproduction prohibited.

Sample Bankruptcy Forms

Form 1, P2 (6-90)   Julius Blumberg, Inc. NYC 10013

Name of Debtor: Robert Paul Debtor and Jane Debtor	Case No. (Court use only)

FILING OF PLAN

For Chapter 9, 11,12 and 13 cases only. Check appropriate box.
- [ ] A copy of debtor's proposed plan dated _____ is attached.
- [ ] Debtor intends to file a plan within the time allowed by statute, rule, or order of the court.

PRIOR BANKRUPTCY CASE FILED WITHIN LAST 6 YEARS (If more than one, attach additional sheet)

Location Where Filed	Case Number	Date Filed
Any City, Any State	80-B-2145	June 1, 1980

PENDING BANKRUPTCY CASE FILED BY ANY SPOUSE, PARTNER, OR AFFILIATE OF THIS DEBTOR (If more than one, attach additional sheet.)

Name of Debtor	Case Number	Date

Relationship	District	Judge

REQUEST FOR RELIEF

Debtor requests relief in accordance with the chapter of title 11, United States Code, specified in this petition.

SIGNATURES

ATTORNEY

x _Allen B. Attorney_   Date August 28, 1991
Signature Allen B. Attorney

INDIVIDUAL /JOINT DEBTOR(S)	CORPORATE OR PARTNERSHIP DEBTOR
I declare under penalty of perjury that the information provided in this petition is true and correct.	I declare under penalty of perjury that the information provided in this petition is true and correct, and that the filing of this petition on behalf of the debtor has been authorized.

x _Robert P. Debtor_
Signature of Debtor   Robert P. Debtor
Date August 28, 1991

x _____
Signature of Authorized Individual

Print or Type Name of Authorized Individual

x _Jane Debtor_
Signature of Joint Debtor   Jane Debtor
Date August 28, 1991

Title of Individual Authorized by Debtor to File this Petition
Date

EXHIBIT "A" (To be completed if debtor is a corporation requesting relief under chapter 11.)
- [ ] Exhibit "A" is attached and made a part of this petition.

TO BE COMPLETED BY INDIVIDUAL CHAPTER 7 DEBTOR WITH PRIMARILY CONSUMER DEBTS (See P L 98-353 § 322)

I am aware that I may proceed under chapter 7,11,12 or 13 of title 11, United States Code, understand the relief available under each such chapter, and choose to proceed under chapter 7 of such title

If I am represented by an attorney, exhibit "B" has been completed

x _Robert P. Debtor_   Date August 28, 1991
Signature of Debtor   Robert P. Debtor

x _Jane Debtor_   Date August 28, 1991
Signature of Joint Debtor   Jane Debtor

EXHIBIT "B" (To be completed by attorney for individual chapter 7 debtor(s) with primarily consumer debts.)

I, the attorney for the debtor(s) named in the foregoing petition, declare that I have informed the debtor(s) that (he, she, or they) may proceed under chapter 7, 11, 12, or 13 of title 11. United States Code, and have explained the relief available under each such chapter.

x _Allen B. Attorney_   Date August 28, 1991
Signature of Attorney   Allen B. Attorney

3089-2 1991 JULIUS BLUMBERG INC . NYC 10013

Forms may be purchased from Julius Blumberg, Inc., NYC 10013, or any of its dealers. Reproduction prohibited.

Sample Bankruptcy Forms

Form B6 (6-90)

Julius Blumberg, Inc. NYC 10013

UNITED STATES BANKRUPTCY COURT   CENTRAL   **DISTRICT OF** ANY STATE

In re: Robert Paul Debtor and Jane Debtor   Debtor(s)   Case No.   (If Known)

See summary below for the list of schedules. Include Unsworn Declaration under Penalty of Perjury at the end.

GENERAL INSTRUCTIONS: Schedules D, E and F have been designed for the listing of each claim only once. Even when a claim is secured only in part, or entitled to priority only in part, it still should be listed only once. A claim which is secured in whole or in part should be listed on Schedule D only, and a claim which is entitled to priority in whole or in part should be listed in Schedule E only. Do not list the same claim twice. If a creditor has more than one claim, such as claims arising from separate transactions, each claim should be scheduled separately.

Review the specific instructions for each schedule before completing the schedule.

SUMMARY OF SCHEDULES

Indicate as to each schedule whether that schedule is attached and state the number of pages in each. Report the totals from Schedules A, B, D, E, F, I and J in the boxes provided. Add the amounts from Schedules A and B to determine the total amount of the debtor's assets. Add the amounts from Schedules D, E, and F to determine the total amount of the debtor's liabilities.

Name of Schedule	Attached (Yes No)	Number of sheets	Assets	Liabilities	Other
A - Real Property	Y	1	None		
B - Personal Property	Y	1	15,600.00		
C - Property Claimed as Exempt	Y	1			
D - Creditors Holding Secured Claims	Y	1		1,000.00	
E - Creditors Holding Unsecured Priority Claims	Y	1		None	
F - Creditors Holding Unsecured Nonpriority Claims	Y	1		13,100.00	
G - Executory Contracts and Unexpired Leases	Y	1			
H - Codebtors	Y	1			
I - Current Income of Individual Debtor(s)	Y	1			2,560.00
J - Current Expenditures of Individual Debtor(s)	Y	1			1,595.00
Total Number of Sheets of All Schedules		10			
Total Assets			15,600.00		
Total Liabilities				14,100.00	

3072 · 1991 JULIUS BLUMBERG, INC. NYC 10013

Forms may be purchased from Julius Blumberg, Inc., NYC 10013, or any of its dealers. Reproduction prohibited.

Sample Bankruptcy Forms

Form B6 A/B, P1(6-90)   Julius Blumberg, Inc. NYC 10013

In re: Robert Paul Debtor and Jane Debtor   Debtor(s)   Case No.   (If known)

SCHEDULE A - REAL PROPERTY

DESCRIPTION AND LOCATION OF PROPERTY	NATURE OF DEBTOR'S INTEREST IN PROPERTY	H W J C	CURRENT MARKET VALUE OF DEBTOR'S INTEREST IN PROPERTY WITHOUT DEDUCTING ANY SECURED CLAIM OR EXEMPTION	AMOUNT OF SECURED CLAIM
None				

Total -> $ None   (Report also on Summary of Schedules.)

SCHEDULE B - PERSONAL PROPERTY

TYPE OF PROPERTY	N O N E	DESCRIPTION AND LOCATION OF PROPERTY	H W J C	CURRENT MARKET VALUE OF DEBTOR'S INTEREST IN PROPERTY WITHOUT DEDUCTING ANY SECURED CLAIM OR EXEMPTION
1. Cash on hand		Petty cash kept for household use	J	200.00
2. Checking, savings or other financial accounts, certificates of deposit, or shares in banks, savings and loan, thrift, building and loan, and homestead associations, or credit unions, brokerage houses, or cooperatives.		Joint checking account #24287-935 with Any State Bank, Any City, Any State	J	1,100.00
3. Security deposits with public utilities, telephone companies, landlords, and others.		Security deposit with Eastern Realty Corp., landlord of apartment in which Debtors reside.	J	450.00
4. Household goods and furnishings including audio, video and computer equipment.		Estimated value of household goods and furnishings	J	1,700.00
5. Books, pictures and other art objects; antiques, stamp, coin, record, tape, compact disc, and other collections or collectibles.		Estimated value of books, pictures and coin collection	J	250.00
6. Wearing apparel.		Estimated value of wearing apparel	H&W	1,000.00
7. Furs and jewelry.		W's costume jewelry and engagement ring and wedding bands (J)	H&W	1,200.00
8. Firearms and sports, photographic, and other hobby equipment		Fishing equipment	H&W	200.00
9. Interests in insurance policies. Name insurance company of each policy and itemize surrender or refund value of each.		H is the holder of a whole life insurance policy with American Life Insurance Co., Policy #114482; face value $50,000.00; beneficiary is W; cash value is $400.00	H	400.00

1991 JULIUS BLUMBERG INC NYC 10013

Forms may be purchased from Julius Blumberg, Inc., NYC 10013, or any of its dealers. Reproduction prohibited.

Sample Bankruptcy Forms

Form B6B, P2 (6-90) Julius Blumberg, Inc. NYC 10013

**SCHEDULE B
PERSONAL PROPERTY**

In re: Robert Paul Debtor and Jane Debtor   Debtor(s)   Case No.   (if known)

TYPE OF PROPERTY	NONE	DESCRIPTION AND LOCATION OF PROPERTY	H W J C	CURRENT MARKET VALUE OF DEBTOR'S INTEREST IN PROPERTY WITHOUT DEDUCTING ANY SECURED CLAIM OR EXEMPTION
10. Annuities. Itemize and name each issuer.	X			
11. Interests in IRA, ERISA, Keogh, or other pension or profit sharing plans. Itemize		Husband has a vested interest in a pension plan at his place of employment ($3,000.00) & Wife holds an IRA savings account at Any County Bank, Any State ($1,000.00).	H&J	4,000.00
12. Stock and interests in incorporated and unincorporated businesses. Itemize.				
13. Interest in partnerships or joint ventures. Itemize.	X	200 shares of Apex United Corp.	J	600.00 (approx.)
14. Government and corporate bonds and other negotiable and nonegotiable instruments.		Series EE U.S. Savings Bonds	W	300.00
15. Accounts receivable.	X			
16. Alimony, maintenance, support, and property settlements to which the debtor is or may be entitled. Give particulars.	X			
17. Other liquidated debts owing debtor including tax refunds. Give particulars.		1990 Federal Income Tax Refund	J	400.00
18. Equitable or future interests, life estates, and rights or powers exercisable for the benefit of the debtor other than those listed in Schedule of Real Property.	X			
19. Contingent and noncontingent interests in estate of a decedent, death benefit plan, life insurance policy, or trust.	X			
20. Other contingent and unliquidated claims of every nature, including tax refunds, counterclaims of the debtor, and rights to setoff claims. Give estimated value of each.		W is the plaintiff in a personal injury action pending in the Circuit Court of Any County, Any State seeking $20,000 for injuries sustained by him in an automobile collision with an automobile driven by Richard Ross.	W	Unknown
21. Patents, copyrights, and other intellectual property. Give particulars	X			
22. Licenses, franchises, and other general intangibles. Give particulars.	X			
23. Automobiles, trucks, trailers, and other vehicles and accessories		Husband owns a 1988 Ford (worth approximately $2,000.00) and Wife owns a 1987 Dodge (worth approximately $1,800.00)	H&J	3,800.00
24. Boats, motors, and accessories	X			
25. Aircraft and accessories.	X			
26. Office equipment, furnishings, and supplies	X			
27. Machinery, fixtures, equipment, and supplies used in business	X			
28. Inventory.	X			
29. Animals.	X			
30. Crops - growing or harvested. Give particulars	X			
31. Farming equipment and implements.	X			
32. Farm supplies, chemicals, and feed	X			
33. Other personal property of any kind not already listed. Itemize.	X			

(Include amounts from any continuation sheets attached. Report total also on Summary of Schedules)   Total -> $ 15,600.00

_____ continuation sheets attached

Forms may be purchased from Julius Blumberg, Inc., NYC 10013, or any of its dealers. Reproduction prohibited.

Sample Bankruptcy Forms

Form B6 C (6,90) Julius Blumberg, Inc. NYC 10013

In re: Robert Paul Debtor and Jane Debtor   Debtor(s)   Case No.   (if known)

SCHEDULE C - PROPERTY CLAIMED AS EXEMPT

Debtor elects the exemptions to which debtor is entitled under (Check one box)

☐ 11 U.S.C. § 522(b)(1): Exemptions provided in 11 U.S.C. § 522(d). Note: These exemptions are available only in certain states.
☒ 11 U.S.C. § 522(b)(2): Exemptions available under applicable nonbankruptcy federal laws, state or local law.

DESCRIPTION OF PROPERTY	SPECIFY LAW PROVIDING EACH EXEMPTION	VALUE OF CLAIMED EXEMPTION	CURRENT MARKET VALUE OF PROPERTY WITHOUT DEDUCTING EXEMPTION
1. Cash (Schedule B-1)	Any State Civil Code Section 524	200.00	200.00
2. Checking account (Schedule B-2)	Any State Civil Code Section 524	1,100.00	1,100.00
3. Security deposit (Schedule B-3)	Any State Civil Code Section 524	450.00	450.00
4. Household goods and furnishings (Schedule B-4)	Any State Civil Code Section 525	1,700.00	1,700.00
5. Books, etc. (Schedule B-5)	Any State Civil Code Section 525	250.00	250.00
6. Wearing apparel (Schedule B-6)	Any State Civil Code Section 525	1,000.00	1,000.00
7. Jewelry (Schedule B-7)	Any State Civil Code Section 525	1,200.00	1,200.00
8. Fishing equipment, etc. (Schedule B-8)	Any State Civil Code Section 525	200.00	200.00
9. Life Insurance (Schedule B-9)	Any State Insurance Law Section 822	400.00	400.00
10. H's pension plan rights (Schedule B-11)	Federal Employees Retirement Income Security Act	3,000.00	3,000.00
11. W's IRA (Schedule B-11)	Any State Civil Code Section 523	1,000.00	1,000.00
12. Savings bonds (Schedule B-14)	Any State Civil Code Section 524	300.00	300.00
13. Income Tax Refund (Schedule B-17)	Any State Civil Code Section 524	400.00	400.00
14. Personal injury action (Schedule B-20)	Any State Civil Code Section 526	Complete recovery	None
15. H's automobile (Schedule B-23)	Any State Civil Code Section 527	2,000.00	2,000.00
16. W's automobile (Schedule B-23)	Any State Civil Code Section 527	1,800.00	1,800.00

Forms may be purchased from Julius Blumberg, Inc., NYC 10013, or any of its dealers. Reproduction prohibited.

Sample Bankruptcy Forms

Form B6 D (6-90)   Julius Blumberg, Inc. NYC 10013

In re: Robert Paul Debtor and Jane Debtor   Debtor(s)   Case No.   (if known)

SCHEDULE D - CREDITORS HOLDING SECURED CLAIMS

CREDITOR'S NAME AND MAILING ADDRESS INCLUDING ZIP CODE	CODEBTOR	H W J C	DATE CLAIM WAS INCURRED, NATURE OF LIEN, AND DESCRIPTION AND MARKET VALUE OF PROPERTY SUBJECT TO LIEN	C U D	AMOUNT OF CLAIM WITHOUT DEDUCTING VALUE OF COLLATERAL	UNSECURED PORTION IF ANY
ACCOUNT NO. 484721 Western Bank 129 Whiting Boulevard Any City, Any State 84132		H	Automobile loan obtained on purchase of 1988 Ford VALUE $ 2,000.00		1,000.00	
ACCOUNT NO.			VALUE $			
ACCOUNT NO.			VALUE $			
ACCOUNT NO.			VALUE $			
ACCOUNT NO.			VALUE $			
ACCOUNT NO.			VALUE $			
ACCOUNT NO.			VALUE $			
ACCOUNT NO.			VALUE $			

_____ continuation sheets attached

Subtotal -> (Total of this page) $

Total -> (use only on last page) $ 1,000.00

(Report total also on Summary of Schedules)

Forms may be purchased from Julius Blumberg, Inc., NYC 10013, or any of its dealers. Reproduction prohibited.

Sample Bankruptcy Forms

Form B6 E (6-90)

Julius Blumberg, Inc NYC 10013

In re Robert Paul Debtor and Jane Debtor   Debtor(s)   Case No   (if known)

SCHEDULE E - CREDITORS HOLDING UNSECURED PRIORITY CLAIMS

[X] Check this box if debtor has no creditors holding unsecured priority claims to report on this Schedule E.

TYPE OF PRIORITY CLAIMS (Check the appropriate box(es) below if claims in that category are listed on the attached sheets)

[ ] **Extensions of credit in an involuntary case**
Claims arising in the ordinary course of the debtor's business or financial affairs after the commencement of the case but before the earlier of the appointment of a trustee or the order for relief 11 U S C § 507(a)(2).

[ ] **Wages, salaries, and commissions**
Wages, salaries, and commissions, including vacation, severance, and sick leave pay owing to employees, up to a maximum of $2000 per employee, earned within 90 days immediately preceding the filing of the original petition, or the cessation of business, whichever occured first, to the extent provided in 11 U S C § 507(a)(3)

[ ] **Contributions to employee benefit plans**
Money owed to employee benefit plans for services rendered within 180 days immediately preceding the filing of the original petition, or the cessation of business, whichever occured first, to the extent provided in 11 U.S.C. § 507(a)(4).

[ ] **Certain farmers and fishermen**
Claims of certain farmers and fishermen, up to a maximum of $2000 per farmer or fisherman, against the debtor, as provided in 11 U.S.C. § 507(a)(5).

[ ] **Deposits by individuals**
Claims of individuals up to a maximum of $900 for deposits for the purchase, lease, or rental of property or services for personal, family, or household use, that were not delivered or provided 11 U S C § 507(a)(6)

[ ] **Taxes and Certain Other Debts Owed to Governmental Units**
Taxes, customs duties, and penalties owing to federal, state, and local governmental units as set forth in 11 U.S.C. § 507(a)(7).

CREDITOR'S NAME AND MAILING ADDRESS INCLUDING ZIP CODE	CODEBT	H W J C	DATE CLAIM WAS INCURRED AND CONSIDERATION FOR CLAIM	C U D	TOTAL AMOUNT OF CLAIM	AMOUNT ENTITLED TO PRIORITY
ACCOUNT NO.						
ACCOUNT NO.						
ACCOUNT NO.						
ACCOUNT NO.						
ACCOUNT NO.						
			Subtotal -> (Total of this page)		$	
Continuation sheets attached			Total -> (use only on last page of the completed Schedule E)		$ (Report total also on Summary of Schedules)	

3072 1991 JULIUS BLUMBERG INC NYC 10013

Forms may be purchased from Julius Blumberg, Inc., NYC 10013, or any of its dealers. Reproduction prohibited.

Sample Bankruptcy Forms

Form B6 F (6-90)

Julius Blumberg, Inc. NYC 10013

In re: Robert Paul Debtor and Jane Debtor   Debtor(s)   Case No.   (If known)

SCHEDULE F - CREDITORS HOLDING UNSECURED NONPRIORITY CLAIMS

☐ Check this box if debtor has no creditors holding unsecured nonpriority claims to report on this Schedule F

CREDITOR'S NAME AND MAILING ADDRESS INCLUDING ZIP CODE	CO DEBT	H W J C	DATE CLAIM WAS INCURRED AND CONSIDERATION FOR CLAIM. IF CLAIM IS SUBJECT TO SETOFF, SO STATE.	C U D	AMOUNT OF CLAIM
ACCOUNT NO. 24866 Inland Magazine, Inc. 400 Madison Avenue Central City, Central State 64584		W	Magazine subscriptions - 1987 & 1988		80.00
ACCOUNT NO. 86214 Zenith Economy Store Corp. 777 Back Street Any City, Any State 80001		J	Miscellaneous purchases in 1988 & 1989		720.00
ACCOUNT NO. 10584 Any City Hospital 246 South Boulevard Any City, Any State 80002		J	Medical services for daughter in 1989		3,200.00
ACCOUNT NO. 7274 Helen Baldwin, MD 927 Orange Road Any City, Any State 82543		J	Medical services for daughter in 1989		2,100.00
ACCOUNT NO. 270052 U.S. Charge A Lot Corp. 999 Money Way North City, North State 28421		J	Credit card charges, at various times in 1987, 1988, 1989 and 1990		4,400.00
ACCOUNT NO. 4182666 ABC Finance Co. 890 Front Street Any City, Any State 82486		H	Balance due in connection with repossessed automobile in 1987		1,700.00
ACCOUNT NO. 511624 Rite-Way Furniture, Inc. 2111 Commerce Avenue Any City, Any State 80042		J	Balance due on installment purchase of furniture purchased in 1988		900.00
ACCOUNT NO.					
ACCOUNT NO.					

_____ Continuation Sheets attached.

Subtotal -> $
(Total of this page)

Total -> $13,100.00
(use only on last page of completed Schedule F.)
(Report total also on Summary of Schedules)

3072 F 1991 JULIUS BLUMBERG, INC. NYC 10013

Forms may be purchased from Julius Blumberg, Inc., NYC 10013, or any of its dealers. Reproduction prohibited.

Sample Bankruptcy Forms

Form B6 G (6-90) Julius Blumberg, Inc. NYC 10013

In re: Robert Paul Debtor and Jane Debtor   Debtor(s)   Case No.   (if known)

SCHEDULE G - EXECUTORY CONTRACTS AND UNEXPIRED LEASES

☐ Check this box if debtor has no executory contracts or unexpired leases.

NAME AND MAILING ADDRESS, INCLUDING ZIP CODE, OF OTHER PARTIES TO LEASE OR CONTRACT.	DESCRIPTION OF CONTRACT OR LEASE AND NATURE OF DEBTOR'S INTEREST. STATE WHETHER LEASE IS FOR NONRESIDENTIAL REAL PROPERTY. STATE CONTRACT NUMBER OF ANY GOVERNMENT CONTRACT.
Eastern Realty Corp. 1842 Walton Avenue Any City, Any State 81472	Apartment lease to apartment no. 6A located at 101 East First Street, Any City, Any State. Term is for two years with the initial term ending on December 31, 1991.

3072 © 1991 JULIUS BLUMBERG, INC. NYC 10013

Forms may be purchased from Julius Blumberg, Inc., NYC 10013, or any of its dealers. Reproduction prohibited.

Sample Bankruptcy Forms

Form B6 H, (6-90) Julius Blumberg, Inc. NYC 10013

In re: Robert Paul Debtor and Jane Debtor   Debtor(s)   Case No.   (If known)

SCHEDULE H - CODEBTORS

☒ Check this box if debtor has no codebtors.

NAME AND ADDRESS OF CODEBTOR	NAME AND ADDRESS OF CREDITOR

226

Sample Bankruptcy Forms

Form 861 (6-90) Julius Blumberg, Inc. NYC 10013

In re Robert Paul Debtor and Jane Debtor   Debtor(s)   Case No.   (if known)

SCHEDULE I - CURRENT INCOME OF INDIVIDUAL DEBTOR(S)

The column labeled "Spouse" must be completed in all cases filed by joint debtors and by a married debtor in a chapter 12 or 13 case whether or not a joint petition is filed, unless the spouses are separated and a joint petition is not filed.

Debtor's Marital Status:	DEPENDENTS OF DEBTOR AND SPOUSE		
	NAMES	AGE	RELATIONSHIP
Married	Allison Debtor	3	Daughter
	Peter M. Debtor	1	Son

Employment:	DEBTOR	SPOUSE
Occupation	Computer Technician	Part-time real estate salesperson
Name of Employer	ABC Company	Able Real Estate Company
How long employed	5 years	7 years
Address of Employer	291 West Street Any City, Any State 82436	238 East Avenue Any City, Any State 82435

Income: (Estimate of average monthly income)   DEBTOR   SPOUSE

Current monthly gross wages, salary, and commissions (pro rate if not paid monthly.)	$ 2,160.00	$ 1,400.00
Estimate monthly overtime		
SUBTOTAL	$ 2,160.00	$ 1,400.00
LESS PAYROLL DEDUCTIONS		
a. Payroll taxes and social security	660.00	300.00
b. Insurance	40.00	
c. Union dues		
d. Other (Specify)		
SUBTOTAL OF PAYROLL DEDUCTIONS	$ 700.00	$ 300.00
TOTAL NET MONTHLY TAKE HOME PAY	$ 1,460.00	$ 1,100.00

Regular income from operation of business or profession or farm
(attach detailed statement)
Income from real property
Interest and dividends
Alimony, maintenance or support payments payable to the debtor for the debtor's
 use or that of dependents listed above
Social security or other government assistance (Specify)

Pension or retirement income
Other monthly income (Specify)

TOTAL MONTHLY INCOME $ 1,460.00 $ 1,100.00

TOTAL COMBINED MONTHLY INCOME $ 2,560.00   (Report also on Summary of Schedules)

Describe any increase or decrease of more than 10% in any of the above categories anticipated to occur within the year following the filing of this document:

3072 · 1991 JULIUS BLUMBERG INC. NYC 10013

Forms may be purchased from Julius Blumberg, Inc., NYC 10013, or any of its dealers. Reproduction prohibited.

Sample Bankruptcy Forms

Form 86 J, Cont. (6-90)   Julius Blumberg, Inc. NYC 10013

In re: Robert Paul Debtor and Jane Debtor   Debtor(s)   Case No.   (if known)

SCHEDULE J - CURRENT EXPENDITURES OF INDIVIDUAL DEBTOR(S)

Complete this schedule by estimating the average monthly expenses of the debtor and the debtor's family. Pro rate any payments made bi-weekly, quarterly, semi-annually, or annually to show monthly rate.

☐ Check this box if a joint petition is filed and debtor's spouse maintains a separate household. Complete a separate schedule of expenditures labeled "Spouse".

Rent or home mortgage payment (include lot rented for mobile home)	$ 500.00
Are real estate taxes included? ☐ Yes ☒ No Is property insurance included? ☐ Yes ☒ No	
Utilities Electricity and heating fuel	
Water and sewer	
Telephone	
Other	50.00
Home maintenance (repairs and upkeep)	
Food	400.00
Clothing	100.00
Laundry and dry cleaning	20.00
Medical and dental expenses	50.00
Transportation (not including car payments)	100.00
Recreation, clubs and entertainment, newspapers, magazines, etc.	
Charitable contributions	25.00
Insurance (not deducted from wages or included in home mortgage payments)	30.00
Homeowner's or renter's	
Life	20.00
Health	30.00
Auto	40.00
Other	120.00
Taxes (not deducted from wages or included in home mortgage payments)	
(Specify)	
Installment payments: (In chapter 12 and 13 cases, do not list payments to be included in the plan)	
Auto	110.00
Other	
Alimony, maintenance, and support paid to others	
Payments for support of additional dependents not living at your home	
Regular expenses from operation of business, profession, or farm (attach detailed statement)	
Other	
TOTAL MONTHLY EXPENSES (Report also on Summary of Schedules)	$ 1,595.00

(FOR CHAPTER 12 AND 13 DEBTORS ONLY)
Provide the information requested below, including whether plan payments are to be made bi-weekly, monthly, annually, or at some other regular interval.

A. Total projected monthly income $
B. Total projected monthly expenses $
C. Excess income (A minus B) $

D. Total amount to be paid into plan each $
                    (interval)

Forms may be purchased from Julius Blumberg, Inc., NYC 10013, or any of its dealers. Reproduction prohibited.

Sample Bankruptcy Forms

Form B6 Cont. (6-90)   Julius Blumberg, Inc. NYC 10013

In re: Robert Paul Debtor and Jane Debtor   Debtor(s)   Case No. _____ (if known)

DECLARATION CONCERNING DEBTOR'S SCHEDULES

DECLARATION UNDER PENALTY OF PERJURY BY INDIVIDUAL DEBTOR

I declare under penalty of perjury that I have read the foregoing summary and schedules, consisting of ____11____ sheets, and that they are true and correct to the best of my knowledge, information, and belief.
(Total shown on summary page plus 1.)

Date August 28, 1991   Signature: _Robert P. Debtor_
                                         Debtor Robert P. Debtor

Date August 28, 1991   Signature: _Jane Debtor_
                                         (Joint Debtor, if any) Jane Debtor
                             (If joint case, both spouses must sign.)

DECLARATION UNDER PENALTY OF PERJURY ON BEHALF OF CORPORATION OR PARTNERSHIP

I, the _____ (the president or other officer or an authorized agent of the corporation or a member or an authorized agent of the partnership) of the _____ (corporation or partnership) named as debtor in this case, declare under penalty of perjury that I have read the foregoing summary and schedules, consisting of _____ sheets, and that they are true and correct to the best of my knowledge, information, and belief.
(Total shown on summary page plus 1.)

Date _____   Signature: _____

(Print or type name of individual signing on behalf of debtor.)

(An individual signing on behalf of a partnership or corporation must indicate position or relationship to debtor.)

Penalty for making a false statement or concealing property: Fine of up to $500,000 or imprisonment for up to 5 years or both. 18 U.S.C. §§ 152 and 3571.

3072 1991 JULIUS BLUMBERG INC NYC 10013

Forms may be purchased from Julius Blumberg, Inc., NYC 10013, or any of its dealers. Reproduction prohibited.

Sample Bankruptcy Forms

Form 7 Stmt of Financial Affairs (8-91)

Julius Blumberg, Inc. NYC 10013

UNITED STATES BANKRUPTCY COURT CENTRAL DISTRICT OF ANY STATE

In re Robert Paul Debtor and Jane Debtor   Debtor(s)   Case No.

STATEMENT OF FINANCIAL AFFAIRS

This statement is to be completed by every debtor. Spouses filing a joint petition may file a single statement on which the information for both spouses is combined. If the case is filed under chapter 12 or chapter 13, a married debtor must furnish information for both spouses whether or not a joint petition is filed, unless the spouses are separated and a joint petition is not filed. An individual debtor engaged in business as a sole proprietor, partner, family farmer, or self-employed professional, should provide the information requested on this statement concerning all such activities as well as the individual's personal affairs.

Questions 1-15 are to be completed by all debtors. Debtors that are or have been in business, as defined below, also must complete Questions 16-21. Each question must be answered. If the answer to any question is "None," or the question is not applicable, mark the box labeled "None." If additional space is needed for the answer to any question, use and attach a separate sheet properly identified with the case name, case number (if known), and the number of the question.

DEFINITIONS

"*In business.*" A debtor is "in business" for the purpose of this form if the debtor is a corporation or partnership. An individual debtor is "in business" for the purpose of this form if the debtor is or has been, within the two years immediately preceding the filing of this bankruptcy case, any of the following: an officer, director, managing executive, or person in control of a corporation; a partner, other than a limited partner, of a partnership; a sole proprietor or self-employed.

"*Insider.*" The term "insider" includes but is not limited to: relatives of the debtor, general partners of the debtor and their relatives; corporations of which the debtor is an officer, director, or person in control; officers, directors, and any person in control of a corporate debtor and their relatives; affiliates of the debtor and insiders of such affiliates; any managing agent of the debtor. 11 U.S.C. §101(30)

☐ None **1. Income from Employment or Operation of Business**

State the gross amount of income the debtor has received from employment, trade, or profession, or from operation of the debtor's business from the beginning of this calendar year to the date this case was commenced. State also the gross amounts received during the two years immediately preceding this calendar year (A debtor that maintains, or has maintained, financial records on the basis of a fiscal rather than a calendar year may report fiscal year.) Identify the beginning and ending dates of the debtor's fiscal year.) If a joint petition is filed, state income for each spouse separately. (Married debtors filing under chapter 12 or chapter 13 must state income of both spouses whether or not a joint petition is filed, unless the spouses are separated and a joint petition is not filed.)
Give AMOUNT and SOURCE (If more than one)

Robert Paul Debtor was engaged in a part-time landscaping business which was terminated in January of 1991. In 1989 he earned $6,500.00 from that business and in 1990 - $5,100.00.

☐ None **2. Income Other than from Employment or Operation of Business**

State the amount of income received by the debtor other than from employment, trade, profession, or operation of the debtor's business during the two years immediately preceding the commencement of this case. Give particulars. If a joint petition is filed, state income for each spouse separately. (Married debtors filing under chapter 12 or chapter 13 must state income for each spouse whether or not a joint petition is filed, unless the spouses are separated and a joint petition is not filed.)
Give AMOUNT and SOURCE

Robert Paul Debtor is a computer technician with ABC Co., 291 West Street, Any City, Any State 82436. His 1989 salary was $23,500.00. His 1990 salary was $24,250.00. Jane Debtor is a part-time real estate salesperson with Able Real Estate Co., 238 East Avenue, Any City, Any State 82435. Her commissions from such employment were $13,800.00 in 1989 and $15,200.00 in 1990.

3. Payments to Creditors

☐ None a. List all payments on loans, installment purchases of goods or services, and other debts, aggregating more than $600 to any creditor, made within 90 days immediately preceding the commencement of this case. (Married debtors filing under chapter 12 or chapter 13 must include payments by either or both spouses whether or not a joint petition is filed, unless the spouses are separated and a joint petition is not filed.)
Give NAME AND ADDRESS OF CREDITOR, DATES OF PAYMENTS, AMOUNT PAID and AMOUNT STILL OWING

Loans-Regular monthly payments made of $216.00 made to Any City Bank on account of personal loan to both Debtors. Installment purchases-none. Other debts - intermittent payments were made in the regular course of Debtors' personal financial affairs to various creditors. Creditors and all such payments are reflected in Debtors' checking account records.

☒ None b. List all payments made within one year immediately preceding the commencement of this case to or for the benefit of creditors who are or were insiders. (Married debtors filing under chapter 12 or chapter 13 must include payments by either or both spouses whether or not a joint petition is filed, unless the spouses are separated and a joint petition is not filed.)
Give NAME AND ADDRESS OF CREDITOR AND RELATIONSHIP TO DEBTOR, DATE OF PAYMENT, AMOUNT PAID and AMOUNT STILL OWING

4. Suits, Executions, Garnishments and Attachments

☐ None a. List all suits to which the debtor is or was a party within one year immediately preceding the filing of this bankruptcy case. (Married debtors filing under chapter 12 or chapter 13 must include information concerning either or both spouses whether or not a joint petition is filed, unless the spouses are separated and a joint petition is not filed.)
Give CAPTION OF SUIT AND CASE NUMBER, NATURE OF PROCEEDING, COURT AND LOCATION and STATUS OR DISPOSITION

☐ None b. Describe all property that has been attached, garnished, or seized under any legal or equitable process within one year

Any State Court of Any County. XYZ Carpet Co. v. Robert Paul Debtor and Jane Debtor. Suit to collect balance due for carpet purchase ($1,350.00). Any City Court, Any City, Any State. Fred Smith, MD v. Jane Debtor. Suit to collect medical bill; settled in October 1990. See also Section 5 below.

Wages of Robert Paul Debtor by XYZ Carpet Co. in

Forms may be purchased from Julius Blumberg, Inc., NYC 10013, or any of its dealers. Reproduction prohibited.

Sample Bankruptcy Forms

immediately preceding the commencement of this case. (Married debtors filing under chapter 12 or chapter 13 must include information concerning property of either or both spouses whether or not a joint petition is filed, unless the spouses are separated and a joint petition is not filed.)
Give NAME AND ADDRESS OF PERSON FOR WHOSE BENEFIT PROPERTY WAS SEIZED. DATE OF SEIZURE and DESCRIPTION AND VALUE OF PROPERTY

☐ None **5. Repossessions, Foreclosures, and Returns**

List all property that has been repossessed by a creditor, sold at a foreclosure sale, transferred through a deed in lieu of foreclosure or returned to the seller, within **one year** immediately preceding the commencement of this case. (Married debtors filing under chapter 12 or chapter 13 must include information concerning property of either or both spouses whether or not a joint petition is filed, unless the spouses are separated and a joint petition is not filed.)
Give NAME AND ADDRESS OF CREDITOR OR SELLER. DATE OF REPOSSESSION, FORECLOSURE SALE, TRANSFER OR RETURN and DESCRIPTION AND VALUE OF PROPERTY

6. Assignments and Receiverships

☒ None a. Describe any assignment of property for the benefit of creditors made within **120 days** immediately preceding the commencement of this case. (Married debtors filing under chapter 12 or chapter 13 must include any assignment by either or both spouses whether or not a joint petition is filed, unless the spouses are separated and a joint petition is not filed.)
Give NAME AND ADDRESS OF ASSIGNEE, DATE OF ASSIGNMENT and TERMS OF ASSIGNMENT OR SETTLEMENT

☒ None b. List all property which has been in the hands of a custodian, receiver, or court-appointed official within **one year** immediately preceding the commencement of this case. (Married debtors filing under chapter 12 or chapter 13 must include information concerning property of either or both spouses whether or not a joint petition is filed, unless the spouses are separated and a joint petition is not filed.)
Give NAME AND ADDRESS OF CUSTODIAN. NAME AND LOCATION OF COURT CASE TITLE & NUMBER, DATE OF ORDER and DESCRIPTION AND VALUE OF PROPERTY

☐ None **7. Gifts**

List all gifts or charitable contributions made within **one year** immediately preceding the commencement of this case except ordinary and usual gifts to family members aggregating less than $200 in value per individual family member and charitable contributions aggregating less than $100 per recipient. (Married debtors filing under chapter 12 or chapter 13 must include gifts or contributions by either or both spouses whether or not a joint petition is filed, unless the spouses are separated and a joint petition is not filed.)
Give NAME AND ADDRESS OF PERSON OR ORGANIZATION. RELATIONSHIP TO DEBTOR, IF ANY. DATE OF GIFT and DESCRIPTION AND VALUE OF GIFT

☐ None **8. Losses**

List all losses from fire, theft, other casualty or gambling within **one year** immediately preceding the commencement of this case or since the commencement of this case. (Married debtors filing under chapter 12 or chapter 13 must include losses by either or both spouses whether or not a joint petition is filed, unless the spouses are separated and a joint petition is not filed.)
Give DESCRIPTION AND VALUE OF PROPERTY DESCRIPTION OF CIRCUMSTANCES AND IF LOSS WAS COVERED IN WHOLE OR IN PART BY INSURANCE. GIVE PARTICULARS and DATE OF LOSS

☐ None **9. Payments Related to Debt Counseling or Bankruptcy**

List all payments made or property transferred by or on behalf of the debtor to any persons, including attorneys, for consultation concerning debt consolidation, relief under the bankruptcy law or preparation of a petition in bankruptcy within **one year** immediately preceding the commencement of this case.
Give NAME AND ADDRESS OF PAYEE, DATE OF PAYMENT. NAME OF PAYOR IF OTHER THAN DEBTOR and AMOUNT OF MONEY OR DESCRIPTION AND VALUE OF PROPERTY

☐ None **10. Other Transfers**

List all other property, other than property transferred in the ordinary course of the business or financial affairs of the debtor, transferred either absolutely or as security within **one year** immediately preceding the commencement of this case. (Married debtors filing under chapter 12 or chapter 13 must include transfers by either or both spouses whether or not a joint petition is filed, unless the spouses are separated and a joint petition is not filed.)
Give NAME AND ADDRESS OF TRANSFEREE, RELATIONSHIP TO DEBTOR. DATE and DESCRIBE PROPERTY TRANSFERRED AND VALUE RECEIVED

case described in Section 4a.

1987 Chevrolet (valued at $1,400.00) repossessed by ABC Finance Co., 890 Front Street, Any City, Any State, 85712 on December 15, 1990.

Debtors contributed a total of $300.00 to their Church's building and family services funds during 1990/1991.

Jane Debtor's 1985 Chrysler was stolen on November 28, 1990. The entire loss was covered by insurance.

See annexed Rule 2016(b) Statement.

Robert Paul Debtor sold his 1986 Ford automobile on April 13, 1991 to Douglas Martin, 22 Rich Drive, Any City, Any State 88422, for $600.00.

Sample Bankruptcy Forms

☐ None **11. Closed Financial Accounts**
List all financial accounts and instruments held in the name of the debtor or for the benefit of the debtor which were closed, sold, or otherwise transferred within one year immediately preceding the commencement of this case. Include checking, savings, or other financial accounts, certificates of deposit, or other instruments; shares and share accounts held in banks, credit unions, pension funds, cooperatives, associations, brokerage houses and other financial institutions (Married debtors filing under chapter 12 or chapter 13 must include information concerning accounts or instruments held by or for either or both spouses whether or not a joint petition is filed, unless the spouses are separated and a joint petition is not filed.)
Give NAME AND ADDRESS OF INSTITUTION, TYPE AND NUMBER OF ACCOUNT AND AMOUNT OF FINAL BALANCE and AMOUNT AND DATE OF SALE OR CLOSING

Joint checking account with Any City Bank, 321 East Division Street, Any City, Any State 85941. Account was #4682-3751. Final balance was $82.00. Account was closed on February 19, 1991.

☐ None **12. Safe Deposit Boxes**
List each safe deposit or other box or depository in which the debtor has or had securities, cash, or other valuables within one year immediately preceding the commencement of this case. (Married debtors filing under chapter 12 or chapter 13 must include boxes or depositories of either or both spouses whether or not a joint petition is filed, unless the spouses are separated and a joint petition is not filed.)
Give NAME AND ADDRESS OF BANK OR OTHER DEPOSITORY, NAMES AND ADDRESSES OF THOSE WITH ACCESS TO BOX OR DEPOSITORY, DESCRIPTION OF CONTENTS and DATE OF TRANSFER OR SURRENDER, IF ANY

Safe deposit box in Any City Bank, 321 East Division Street, Any City, Any State 84711; only the Debtors have right of access; contains wills, insurance policies and other personal papers.

☐ None **13. Setoffs**
List all setoffs made by any creditor, including a bank, against a debt or deposit of the debtor within **90 days** preceding the commencement of this case. (Married debtors filing under chapter 12 or chapter 13 must include information concerning either or both spouses whether or not a joint petition is filed, unless the spouses are separated and a joint petition is not filed.)
Give NAME AND ADDRESS OR CREDITOR, DATE OF SETOFF and AMOUNT OF SETOFF

Debt for personal loan in the amount of $482.00 was setoff by the Any City Bank, 321 East Division Street, Any City, Any State 84711 against funds of Debtors in checking account on September 11, 1990.

☐ None **14. Property Held for Another Person**
List all property owned by another person that the debtor holds or controls.
Give NAME AND ADDRESS OF OWNER, DESCRIPTION AND VALUE OF PROPERTY and LOCATION OF PROPERTY

Jane Debtor is custodian for the parties' daughter, Allison (age 3) of a college education savings account established for her by her grandparents, with the Any City Bank, 321 East Division Street, Any City, Any State 84711, Account #42989-421 with a present balance of $1600.

☐ None **15. Prior Address of Debtor**
If the debtor has moved within the two years immediately preceding the commencement of this case, list all premises which the debtor occupied during that period and vacated prior to the commencement of this case. If a joint petition is filed, report also any separate address of either spouse.
Give ADDRESS, NAME USED and DATES OF OCCUPANCY

819 Juniper Street, Any City, Any State 84110 (1979-1984).

Unsworn Declaration under Penalty of Perjury.

I declare under penalty of perjury that I have read the answers contained in the foregoing statement of financial affairs and any attachments thereto and that they are true and correct.

Date __August 28, 1991__ Signature of Debtor _____
                                                Robert P. Debtor

Date __August 28, 1991__ Signature of Joint Debtor (if any) _____
                                                Jane Debtor

_____ continuation sheets attached

Penalty for making a false statement: Fine of up to $500,000 or imprisonment for up to 5 years, or both. 18 U.S.C. §§152 and 3571

Forms may be purchased from Julius Blumberg, Inc., NYC 10013, or any of its dealers. Reproduction prohibited.

Sample Bankruptcy Forms

Form B8 (6-90)   Julius Blumberg, Inc. NYC 10013

UNITED STATES BANKRUPTCY COURT   CENTRAL   DISTRICT OF   ANY STATE

In re: Robert Paul Debtor and Jane Debtor   Debtor(s)   Case No.
                                                              Chapter

CHAPTER 7 INDIVIDUAL DEBTOR'S STATEMENT OF INTENTION

1. ~~I~~ We the debtor(s) have filed a schedule of assets and liabilities which includes consumer debts secured by property of the estate.
2. ~~My intention~~ Our intention with respect to the property of the estate which secures those consumer debts is as follows:

   a. *Property to Be Surrendered.*

Description of property	Creditor's name	H, W or J

   b. *Property to Be Retained (Specify Reaff'd, Red'd or Exempt to state debtor's intention concerning reaffirmation, redemption, or lien avoidance*.)*

Description of property	Creditor's name	Reaff'd Red'd Exempt
1988 Ford	Western Bank 129 Whiting Boulevard Any City, Any State 84132	Reaffirmed and Fully Exempt

3. I understand that § 521(2)(B) of the Bankruptcy Code requires that I perform the above stated intention within 45 days of the filing of this statement with the court, or within such additional time as the court, for cause, within such 45-day period fixes.

Date August 28, 1991

Robert P. Debtor
Signature of Debtor

Jane Debtor
Signature of Debtor

* Reaff'd - Debt will be reaffirmed pursuant to § 524(c)
  Red'd - Property is claimed as exempt and will be redeemed pursuant to § 722
  Exempt - Lien will be avoided pursuant to § 522(f) and property will be claimed as exempt

Forms may be purchased from Julius Blumberg, Inc., NYC 10013, or any of its dealers. Reproduction prohibited.

Sample Bankruptcy Forms

3085 Statement of compensation: Rule 2016(b), 8-91

UNITED STATES BANKRUPTCY COURT   CENTRAL   **DISTRICT OF** ANY STATE

In re Robert Paul Debtor and Jane Debtor   Debtor(s)   Case No.   (If Known)

STATEMENT
Pursuant to Rule 2016(b)

The undersigned, pursuant to Rule 2016(b) Bankruptcy Rules, states that:

(1) The undersigned is the attorney for the debtor(s) in this case.
(2) The compensation paid or agreed to be paid by the debtor(s) to the undersigned is:
    (a) for legal services rendered or to be rendered in contemplation of and in connection with this case $ 1,000.00
    (b) prior to filing this statement, debtor(s) have paid $ 1,000.00
    (c) the unpaid balance due and payable is $ —
(3) X All of the filing fee in this case has been paid.
(4) The services rendered or to be rendered include the following:
    (a) analysis of the financial situation, and rendering advice and assistance to the debtor(s) in determining whether to file a petition under title 11 of the United States Code.
    (b) preparation and filing of the petition, schedules, statement of affairs and other documents required by the court.
    (c) representation of the debtor(s) at the meeting of creditors.

(5) The source of payments made by the debtor(s) to the undersigned was from earnings, wages and compensation for services performed, ~~any~~

(6) The source of payments to be made by the debtor(s) to the undersigned for the unpaid balance remaining, if any, will be from earnings, wages and compensation for services performed, ~~any~~

(7) The undersigned has received no transfer, assignment or pledge of property ~~except the following for the value stated~~:

(8) The undersigned has not shared or agreed to share with any other entity, other than with members of undersigned's law firm, any compensation paid or to be paid ~~except as follows~~.

Dated: August 28, 1991   Respectfully submitted, *Allen B. Attorney*   Attorney for Petitioner
Allen B. Attorney
Attorney's name and address 541 East Eighth Street, Any City, Any State 83872 (909) 846-5283

© 1991 JULIUS BLUMBERG, INC., NYC 10013

Forms may be purchased from Julius Blumberg, Inc., NYC 10013, or any of its dealers. Reproduction prohibited.

Index

Actuarial method, 19
Alabama, exemptions in, 122
  homestead, 174
Alaska, exemptions in, 123
  homestead, 174
American Bankruptcy Institute (ABI), 185
Arizona, exemptions in, 123–24
  homestead, 174
Arkansas, exemptions in, 125
  homestead, 174
Assets, protection of
  advantage of bankruptcy, 74–75
  basic rules of, 188–89
  conversion of nonexempt property, 190, 191–94
  credit cards, 196–97
  move to another state, 70, 190
  pig theory of, 189–90
  pre-bankruptcy planning and, 189
  sale of nonexempt property, 194–95
  See also Exemptions
Assignment for benefit of creditors, 48
Attachments, 42–43, 76

Attorney, bankruptcy, 10, 81, 105, 180–81
  advisory role of, 181–82
  consultation fee of, 186
  as negotiator, 53, 182–83
  referrals to, 184–85
  as representative, 183–84
  selecting, 185–87
Automatic stay provision, 76, 77, 89, 92–93, 108, 112
Automobile
  exemption, 42, 213
  secured loan, 206

"Badges of fraud," 193
Bankruptcy
  advantages of, 5–6, 9–10, 66–69, 74–79
  case studies of, 11–16
  corporate, 77, 78
  credit after. *See* Credit, reestablishing
  credit file record of, 30, 198–99
  disadvantages of, 79–84
  dischargeable debt in. *See* Assets,

235

Index

Bankruptcy (*continued*)
    protection of; Exemptions
    do-it-yourself, 53, 85, 180
    increase in, 69, 77–78
    nondischargeable debt in, 71–73
    previous, 4
    psychological/emotional aspects of, 81, 83, 182
    reasons against filing, 41–46
    warning signs of, 6–9
    See also Bankruptcy law
Bankruptcy Act of 1898, 4
Bankruptcy code. *See* Bankruptcy law
Bankruptcy courts, role of, 5–6
Bankruptcy law
    automatic stay provision of, 76, 77, 89, 92–93, 108, 112
    chapters of, 85–88. *See also* Chapter 7 bankruptcy; Chapter 11 bankruptcy; Chapter 12 bankruptcy; Chapter 13 bankruptcy
    history of, 2–3, 4
    purpose of, 5
    See also Exemptions
Bankruptcy Reform Act of 1978, 4
Banks
    debit cards of, 205–206
    passbook loans of, 205
    secured credit cards of, 204
    See also Credit cards
Best interest test, 108
Billing disputes, 20, 30–32
Billing errors, 31

Chandler Act, 4
Chapter 7 bankruptcy, 45, 79, 82–83, 86, 87, 88, 89–100, 106, 107
    asset/no-asset cases, 95–96
    creditor meeting, 93–95
    creditor notification, 92–93
    discharged debts, 96
    dismissal, 96–97
    eligibility for, 90
    filing, 90–92
    secured creditors, 97–100
    selecting, 90
    trustee role in, 92
Chapter 11 bankruptcy, 42, 43, 78, 86, 101–105, 108
    advantages of, 102
    eligibility for, 101
    filing, 103
    for individuals, 102
    repayment plan, 103–105
Chapter 12 bankruptcy, 42, 43, 86, 101, 106–108
    advantages of, 107
    co-signer protection, 107–108
    eligibility for, 107
    farm debt and, 106
    repayment plan, 108
Chapter 13 bankruptcy, 42, 43, 45, 70, 86–87, 88, 101, 104, 106, 109-20
    advantages of, 111–12
    confirmation hearing, 118
    creditor meeting, 117
    creditor notification, 116
    disadvantages of, 112–13
    discharged debts, 119–20
    eligibility for, 113–14
    employer notification, 115–16
    filing, 114–15
    reasons for selecting, 109–11
    repayment plan, 112, 114, 116–17, 120
    trustee role, 115
Child support, 71, 77, 112
Citibank, 201–202
Collateral, 97–98
Collection agencies, 32–36

Index

cost to creditor, 61–62
debtor protection and, 21–22, 34–36
illegal activities of, 21, 33–34
legal activities of, 21, 33
Colorado, exemptions in, 128–29
homestead, 175
Connally, John, 78
Connecticut, exemptions in, 129, 175, 212
Constitution, U.S., 4, 69
Consultation fee, 186
Consumer Credit Counseling Services, 50–52
Consumer protection laws, 18–22
Consumer report, 24–25, 81
Consumer reporting agencies. *See* Credit agencies/bureaus; Credit file
Corporate bankruptcy, 77, 78
Co-signers, 45, 107–108, 110, 112
Court judgments, 71
Credit
 acceptance of, 3–4, 78–79, 84
 addiction, 13–14
 application, 20, 22–23
 bankruptcy history and, 82–83
 fraud, 45–46, 72, 73, 91, 110
 growth of, 13, 48–49
 refusal of, 20, 21, 27–28, 81
 standing, 81, 112, 113
 See also Loans
Credit, reestablishing, 199–207
 with bank account, 205–206
 with credit cards, 200–204
 credit file and, 206–207
 credit repair clinics and, 207
 with secured laons, 206
Credit agencies/bureaus
 major, 22
 requesting credit report, 28
 requesting file correction, 29
 sale of information, 24–25, 81
 See also Credit file
Credit cards
 lifestyle, 13
 as nondischargeable debt, 73
 preapproved, 201–202
 protection of, during bankruptcy, 197–98, 200–201
 secured, 202–204
Credit counseling services, 50–52, 67
Credit file, 20–21
 bankruptcy information in, 30, 81–82, 198–199
 checking, 25–26, 206–207
 correcting, 28–30, 57
 errors in, 26–27
 kinds of information in, 22–24
 negative information in, 57
 requesting copy of, 28
 statement of dispute in, 29–30
Creditors
 attorney of, 183
 in bankrutpcy process, 75
 and billing disputes, 20, 30–32
 and Chapter 7 bankruptcy, 92–95
 and Chapter 11 bankruptcy, 104
 and Chapter 12 bankruptcy, 108
 and collection agencies, 61–62
 effects of debtor failure on, 59–60
 harrassment by, 74
 legal action by, 75–77
 meeting of, 93–95, 117
 notification of, 92–93, 116, 196
 out-of-court settlement with, 45, 46–48, 54–65
 See also Repayment plan; Secured creditors
Credit repair clinics, 207
Credit Research Center, 199

Index

Debit cards, 205–206
Debt, dischargeable. *See* Exemptions
Debt, nondischargeable. *See* Nondischargeable debt
Debt adjustment services, 49–50
Debt collectors. *See* Collection agencies
Debt counseling
  attorney role in, 52–53, 67, 85 181–182
  by consumer counseling services, 50–52, 67
  by debt adjusters, 49–50
Debtor protection rules. *See* Exemptions
Debtor rights
  under consumer protection laws, 18–22
  consumer reporting and, 22–32
  debt collectors and, 32–36
  Internal Revenue Service (IRS) and, 36–39
Delaware, exemptions in, 130, 175
Diner's Club, 201, 202
Disbursing agent, 48
Dischargeable debt. *See* Exemptions
Discharged debt, 44, 89–90, 96, 118–20
  hardship, 112, 120
Disclosure statement, 18–19, 37, 104
Dismissal, 96–97
Disposable income, 54–55, 117
District of Columbia, exemptions in, 130–131
  homestead, 175
Do-it-yourself bankruptcy, 53, 85, 180
Driver's license, 77

Employment/employer
  and collections agency, 21, 33
  in credit file, 23
  discrimination by, 10
  notification under Chapter 13, 115–16
  and salary garnishment, 14, 75–76, 92
Equal Credit Opportunity Act, 19–20
Exemptions
  conversion of nonexempt property, 190, 191–94
  definition of, 79–80, 192
  under federal law, 122, 212–214
  homestead, 43, 70, 173–79, 213
  under state laws, 69–70, 121–72

Fair Credit Billing Act, 20
Fair Credit Reporting Act, 20, 31
Fair Debt Collection Practices Act, 21–22
Farm debt. *See* Chapter 12 bankruptcy
Federal bankruptcy exemptions, 212–14
Federal Deposit Insurance Corporation (FDIC), 204
Federal Trade Commission, 35
Florida, exemptions in, 69–70, 131–32
  homestead, 175
Fraud
  conversion of nonexempt property and, 193
  credit, 45–46, 72, 73, 91, 110

Gardner, Stephen, 22
Garnishment, 14, 75–76, 92
Georgia, exemptions in, 3, 132–33
  homestead, 175
Government fines/penalties, 71

Hardship discharge, 13, 112, 120

Index

Hawaii, exemptions in, 133, 212
  homestead, 175
Home
  attachment of, 42–43
  mortgage, in bankruptcy process, 43–44, 80
  sale of, 70, 190
  See also Homestead exemption
Home State Savings Bank, 70
Homestead exemption, 43, 70, 173–79, 213
Hunt, H. L., 78

Idaho, exemptions in, 134–35
  homestead, 175
Illinois, exemptions in, 135–36
  homestead, 175
Indiana, exemptions in, 136
  homestead, 176
Internal Revenue Service (IRS), 36–39
  disclosure statement of, 37
  penalties by, 36, 38
  Problem Resolution Office, 39
  restrictions on, 38, 39
  and taxpayer rights, 38–39
Iowa, exemptions in, 137–38
  homestead, 176

Judgment proof designation, 44–45

Kansas, exemptions in, 138
  homestead, 176
Kentucky, exemptions in, 139
  homestead, 176
Kuhn, Bowie, 70

Loans
  cancelling, 19
  co-signed, 45
  mortgage, 42–44, 80–81
  passbook, 205
  secured, 206
Louisiana, exemptions in, 140
  homestead, 176
Luxury goods and services, 192

Mailing, return receipt requested, 21, 28, 31–32
Maine, exemptions in, 140–42
  homestead, 176
Married couples
  under Chapter 7 bankruptcy, 90, 91
  under Chapter 13 bankruptcy, 114, 115
Maryland, exemptions in, 142, 176
Massachusetts, exemptions in, 143, 212
  homestead, 176
MasterCard, 201, 202, 203, 204
Michigan, exemptions in, 143–44, 212
  homestead, 176
Minnesota, exemptions in, 144–45, 212
  homestead, 176
Mississippi, exemptions in, 146–47
  homestead, 176
MoneyCard Systems, 204
Montana, exemptions in, 147–48
  homestead, 177
Mortgage loan, status in bankruptcy, 42–44, 80–81

National Foundation for Consumer Credit, 48
Nebraska, exemptions in, 148–49
  homestead, 177
Nelson, Willie, 36
Nevada, exemptions in, 149–50
  homestead, 177

Index

New Hampshire, exemptions in, 150–51
  homestead, 177
New Jersey, exemptions in, 151, 212
  homestead, 177
New Mexico, exemptions in, 151–52, 212
  homestead, 177
New York, exemptions in, 152–53
  homestead, 177
Nondischargeable debt, 45–45, 71–73
  payment by sale of nonexempt assets, 194–95
Nonexempt assets
  conversion to exempt, 190, 191–194
  sale of, 194–95
North Carolina, exemptions in, 153–54
  homestead, 177
North Dakota, exemptions in, 154–55
  homestead, 177

Ohio, exemptions in, 70, 155–56
  homestead, 177
Oklahoma, exemptions in, 156–57
  homestead, 177
Oregon, exemptions in, 157–58
  homestead, 177–78
Out-of-court settlement, 45, 46–48, 54–65

Payment plan. *See* Repayment plan
Pennsylvania, exemptions in, 158–59, 178, 212
Pig theory, 189–90

Reaffirmation agreement, 98–100
Repayment plan
  Chapter 11 bankruptcy and, 103–105
  Chapter 12 bankruptcy and, 108
  Chapter 13 bankruptcy and, 112, 114, 116–17, 120
  negotiated reduction, 45, 46–48, 54–65, 67
  sale of nonexempt property, 194–95
Repossessions, 76, 99–100, 111, 206
Required property, 192
Return receipt requested, 21, 28, 31–32
Rhode Island, exemptions in, 159–60, 178, 212
Roman Law of the Twelve Tables, 68

Salary, garnishment, 14, 75–76, 92
Sears, Roebuck and Company, 199
Secured credit cards, 202–204
Secured creditors, 41–42, 75
  of automobile loans, 42
  Chapter 12 bankruptcy and, 108
  Chapter 13 bankruptcy and, 113, 119
  collateral and, 97–98
  mortgage holders, 42–44, 80–81
  reaffirmation agreement, 98–100
Secured loans, 206
South Carolina, exemptions in, 160–61
  homestead, 178
South Dakota, exemptions in, 161–62
  homestead, 178
Spousal support, 71, 77, 112
Statement of dispute, 29–30
Student loans, 71
Szczebak, Frank, 199

Taxes, 71, 102, 192
  See also Internal Revenue Service

Index

Tennessee, exemptions in, 162–63
  homestead, 178
Texas, exemptions in, 69, 163–64, 212
  homestead, 178
Trustee, bankruptcy, 92, 115
Truth in Lending Act, 18–19

Uniform Fraudulent Conveyance Act, 193
Unsecured debt, 112, 113, 114, 117
Utah, exemptions in, 164–65
  homestead, 178

Vermont, exemptions in, 165–66, 212
  homestead, 178
Virginia, exemptions in, 166–67
  homestead, 178–79

VISA card, 201–202, 203, 204

Warner, Marvin, 70
Washington, exemptions in, 168, 212
  homestead, 179
West Virginia, exemptions in, 169–70
  homestead, 179
Wisconsin, exemptions in, 170–71, 212
  homestead, 179
Wyoming, exemptions in, 171–72
  homestead, 179

Zaretsky, Barry L., 189

www.ingramcontent.com/pod-product-compliance
Lightning Source LLC
Chambersburg PA
CBHW020740180526
45163CB00001B/294